Access to History

General Editor: Keith Randell

The Civil Wars 1640-9

Access to History

General Editor: Keith Randell

The Civil Wars 1640-9

Angela Anderson

Hodder & Stoughton

A MEMBER OF THE HODDER HEADLINE GROUP

The cover illustration is a portrait of Henry Ireton, attributed to Robert Walker after S. Cooper (by courtesy of the National Portrait Gallery, London).

Some other titles in the series:

The Early Stuarts   ISBN 0 340 57510 7
Katherine Brice

The Interregnum   ISBN 0 340 58207 3
Michael Lynch

Stuart Economy and Society   ISBN 0 340 59703 8
Nigel Heard

Charles V: Ruler, Dynast and Defender of the Faith   ISBN 0 340 53558 X
Stewart MacDonald

Louis XIV, France and Europe 1661-1715   ISBN 0 340 57511 5
Richard Wilkinson

Order queries: Please contact Bookpoint Ltd, 39 Milton Park, Abingdon, Oxon OX14 4TD. Telephone: (44) 01235 400414. Fax: (44) 01235 400454. Lines are open from 9 am - 6 pm Monday to Saturday, with a 24-hour message answering service. Email address: orders@bookpoint.co.uk

British Library Cataloguing in Publication Data

Anderson, Angela
    Civil Wars, 1640-49. – (Access to
    History Series)
    I. Title   II. Series
    941.062

ISBN 0 340 61890 6

First published 1995
Impression number   10 9 8 7 6 5 4
Year   2004 2003 2002 2001 2000 1999 1998

Typeset by Sempringham Publishing Services, Bedford.
Printed in Great Britain for Hodder & Stoughton Educational, a division of Hodder Headline Plc, 338, Euston Road, London NW1 3BH by Redwood Books, Trowbridge, Wiltshire.

Contents

CHAPTER 1 Introduction: Outline of Events, 1530-1649   1
  1 The Origins of Crisis   2
  2 The Road to War   5
  3 From Civil War to Republic   7
  4 Postscript - from Republic to Restoration   9
  Study Guides   10

CHAPTER 2 Interpretations of the Civil Wars   12
  1 History, Politics and the Civil Wars   12
  2 Early Interpretations of the Civil Wars   15
  3 The 'Standard' Whig Interpretation   16
  4 The 'Marxist' School   19
  5 Recent Interpretations of the Civil War   22
  Study Guides   25

CHAPTER 3 From Crisis to Conflict, 1640-2   27
  1 Introduction   27
  2 Actions and Intentions, November 1640-May 1641   29
  3 The First Turning-point: the Death of Strafford   40
  4 The Loss of Parliamentary Unity, May 1641-
    January 1642   41
  5 The Second Turning-point: The Irish Rebellion   51
  6 Conclusion: From Crisis to Conflict   56
  Study Guides   57

CHAPTER 4 A Nation Divided, 1642-3   62
  1 The Process of Division   62
  2 The Nature of Division   64
  3 Assessment - A Nation Divided?   78
  Study Guides   79

CHAPTER 5 The Victory of Parliament, 1643-6   83
  1 The Failure of the Royalists   83
  2 The Assets of Parliament   86
  3 The Achievement of Victory   89
  4 The Resurgence of Neutralism, 1644-5   94
  5 Conclusion - The Victory of Parliament   98
  Study Guides   99

CHAPTER 6 The Emergence of the Radicals   104
  1 The Origins of Radicalism   104
  2 The Parliamentary Search for Settlement   109
  3 Army, Parliament and King, June-November 1647   114
  4 The Leveller Challenge, July-November 1647   117

5 Conclusion - The Emergence of the Radicals   122
Study Guides   123

CHAPTER 7 The Execution of the King, 1648-9   127
    1 The Second Civil War and the Execution of the King 127
    2 Study Guides - Why was Charles I executed in 1649? 137
    3 Conclusion: 'Why was Charles I executed in 1649?'   138

CHAPTER 8 Conclusion: a British Revolution?   146
    Study Guides   149

    Appendix: Comparative Chart of the Main Peace
                Terms   150

    Chronological Table   151

    Further Reading   155

    Index   159

Preface

To the general reader

Although the *Access to History* series has been designed with the needs of students studying the subject at higher examination levels very much in mind, it also has a great deal to offer the general reader. The main body of the text (i.e. ignoring the Study Guides at the ends of chapters) forms a readable and yet stimulating survey of a coherent topic as studied by historians. However, each author's aim has not merely been to provide a clear explanation of what happened in the past (to interest and inform): it has also been assumed that most readers wish to be stimulated into thinking further about the topic and to form opinions of their own about the significance of the events that are described and discussed (to be challenged). Thus, although no prior knowledge of the topic is expected on the reader's part, she or he is treated as an intelligent and thinking person throughout. The author tends to share ideas and possibilities with the reader, rather than passing on numbers of so-called 'historical truths'.

To the student reader

There are many ways in which the series can be used by students studying History at a higher level. It will, therefore, be worthwhile thinking about your own study strategy before you start your work on this book. Obviously, your strategy will vary depending on the aim you have in mind, and the time for study that is available to you.

If, for example, you want to acquire a general overview of the topic in the shortest possible time, the following approach will probably be the most effective:

1 Read Chapter 1 and think about its contents.
2 Read the 'Making notes' section at the end of Chapter 2 and decide whether it is necessary for you to read this chapter.
3 If it is, read the chapter, stopping at each heading to note down the main points that have been made.
4 Repeat stage 2 (and stage 3 where appropriate) for all the other chapters.

If, however, your aim is to gain a thorough grasp of the topic, taking however much time is necessary to do so, you may benefit from carrying out the same procedure with each chapter, as follows:

1 Read the chapter as fast as you can, and preferably at one sitting.
2 Study the flow diagram at the end of the chapter, ensuring that you understand the general 'shape' of what you have just read.

3 Read the 'Making notes' section (and the 'Answering essay questions' section, if there is one) and decide what further work you need to do on the chapter. In particularly important sections of the book, this will involve reading the chapter a second time and stopping at each heading to think about (and to write a summary of) what you have just read.

4 Attempt the 'Source-based questions' section. It will sometimes be sufficient to think through your answers, but additional understanding will often be gained by forcing yourself to write them down.

When you have finished the main chapters of the book, study the 'Further Reading' section and decide what additional reading (if any) you will do on the topic.

This book has been designed to help make your studies both enjoyable and successful. If you can think of ways in which this could have been done more effectively, please write to tell me. In the meantime, I hope that you will gain greatly from your study of History.

Keith Randell

Acknowledgements

The Publishers would like to thank the following for permission to reproduce illustrations in this volume:

Cover - Henry Ireton, attributed to Robert Walker after Samuel Cooper, The National Portrait Gallery, London.

p. 46 (both) the British Museum; p. 95 (top) Mansell Collection (bottom) Fotomas Index; p. 109 British Museum/Fotomas Index; p. 120 The British Library; p. 136 The Earl of Rosebery/The National Galleries of Scotland.

Every effort has been made to trace and acknowledge ownership of copyright. The Publishers will be glad to make suitable arrangements with any copyright holders whom it has not been possible to contact.

CHAPTER 1

Introduction: Outline of Events, 1530-1649

On 30 January 1649 King Charles I was executed at Whitehall in London, having been tried in public for treason against his realm and people. In the following days parliament declared that the monarchy had been discontinued, and within three months it had been formally abolished. A republic was established to replace it. Although individual monarchs had been forcibly removed, and would be again, this remarkable sequence of events remains the only occasion on which an entire political régime has been overthrown by force in Britain. It was a revolution.

The aim of this book is to explore how and why the monarchy fell at the end of what is normally referred to as the English Civil War. The task is a complex one. The student has two main difficulties to overcome when tackling this topic. The first is the mass of factual information that has to be mastered before a start can be made on the central undertaking of thinking about what happened and attempting to make sense of it. The second is the fact that historians over the centuries have disagreed violently over both the causes of what happened and the significance of the events themselves. This means that there is a large amount of historiographical background to be assimilated before any worthwhile independent thinking can be begun.

This dual problem has essentially dictated the structure of the entire book. The first two chapters are effectively introductory: one chapter is devoted to each of the 'factual-overload' and 'conflicting interpretations' difficulties. The remaining chapters seek to develop the outline provided in chapters 1 and 2, by considering some of the issues and events of the period 1640-9 which are thought by historians to be important. The final chapter addresses two of the major sources of debate about this period - the question of how far these events constituted a revolution, and the issue of whether such a revolution should be seen in an English or a British context. It is hoped that by the time the final chapter is reached, the reader will feel sufficiently confident of his or her grasp of the topic to be able to draw some independent conclusions.

The first step must be to form a clear mental picture of the chronological 'shape' of the topic. This is best done by becoming aware of the events that historians have traditionally considered to be central to any study of the subject, and of the way in which they link together to form a core narrative. This chapter is designed to help bring about this awareness. Because the origins of the war have been seen as lying in religious divisions as well as in the growing aspirations of parliament, the chapter begins with the religious reformation of the 1530s. It should be read as quickly as is possible while understanding (rather than memorising) the story that is being presented. It is important that this understanding is then reinforced. The guidance section at the end of the chapter should help to ensure that this is done.

1 The Origins of Crisis

The Reformation in England is symbolised by two events above all. The Act of Supremacy of 1534 gave Henry VIII supreme power over the doctrine and organisation of the Church, which had until then owed loyalty to the Pope as part of the Roman Catholic Church. It made his power legally enforceable by Act of Parliament, thus enhancing the power and status of both parliament and king. The dissolution of the monasteries in 1536-9 transferred most of the wealth of the Church into the hands of the laity (non-churchmen). Following these changes, the intensely personal and Bible-based Protestant faith spread in England, encouraging a more educated and articulate laity, creating religious division as people reached different conclusions from their study of the Bible, and giving the monarch the responsibility for deciding between the conflicting views and claims. In addition, the gradual sale and distribution of Church land helped to create a wealthier and more numerous class of gentry, whose natural political outlet lay in parliament, and in particular, in the House of Commons.

After 30 years of religious changes, mainly enacted through parliament, the Elizabethan Settlement of 1559 sought to create peace by establishing a middle way between Catholic and Protestant ideas, combining Protestant doctrines with more traditional ceremonies and organisation. It was acceptable to the majority, but came under attack from minorities at both ends of the religious spectrum. Catholic plots against the queen and the threat of Spanish invasion combined to create strong anti-Catholic feeling. This was fuelled by memories of the burning of Protestants by Queen Mary (1553-8) and Foxe's *Acts and Monuments,* which recounted the story of their martyrdom, became essential reading for English Protestants after its publication in 1563. This also increased support for the extreme Protestant minority whose demands for further purification of the Church gave them the nickname of 'puritan'.

Frustrated by the queen's opposition to further change, these puritans turned to their sympathisers in parliament, who introduced legislation to reform the Church in various ways. These schemes were based on the ideas published by Thomas Cartwright (a Cambridge scholar) in 1570, which envisaged a Presbyterian system for the Church. Control of the Church would be in the hands of parish ministers who were to be chosen by their congregations and who would maintain discipline with the help of lay supporters (Elders). A similar system had been developed by John Calvin in Geneva and established in Scotland by John Knox in 1568. To the anger of puritan MPs who claimed that parliament had a right to debate such matters, these bills were vetoed by the queen, who was determined to maintain political control of the Church through her appointees, the bishops. For much the same reason, James I upheld this Anglican system when he succeeded to the English throne in 1603. Thus puritanism was contained. But it was not destroyed, and hopes of further reform continued to motivate a minority who were particularly vocal in parliament.

James I succeeded to the throne in 1603, inheriting these religious difficulties and rather more severe financial problems, which were increased by his tendency towards extravagance. He continued Elizabeth's unpopular practice of selling monopoly licences (giving an exclusive right to trade in certain goods) until parliament passed an Act against monopolies in 1624. His attempts to add to his revenue by increasing customs duties led to clashes with parliament. In 1608 a new Book of Rates was published, leading to protests when parliament met in 1610. These unresolved difficulties caused parliament to refuse to grant the customary lifetime right to collect Tunnage and Poundage (customs duties) to Charles I upon his accession in 1625.

This dispute got the new reign off to a bad start, and it went rapidly from bad to worse. Charles persuaded parliament to support a war against Spain in 1625 after he and his father's friend and favourite, George Villiers, Duke of Buckingham, had been humiliated in a fruitless attempt to arrange a marriage with the Infanta (a Spanish princess). Instead, Buckingham, who was now firmly established as Charles's favourite, negotiated a marriage for Charles with Henrietta Maria, the Catholic sister of the King of France. A condition of the marriage was that Charles would allow the queen free exercise of her religion at Court. Within a year, a dispute over shipping had led to war with France, and the new parliament of 1626, infuriated by Buckingham's inept handling of affairs, threatened to impeach him. Charles dissolved parliament in order to protect his friend. This early dissolution deprived Charles of supplies (money) and prevented a resolution of the dispute over Tunnage and Poundage. Charles continued to collect these duties and raised more money by demanding forced loans; those who refused to pay were imprisoned. In 1627 the Five Knights Case supported the legality of this action, but led parliament to present The Petition of Right when it reassembled in 1628. This declared illegal the imprisonment of men without proper cause shown, and the collection of taxes without parliamentary consent. MPs also renewed their attacks on Buckingham, whose expedition to La Rochelle in support of French Protestants in 1627 had ended in costly failure. To protect his favourite, Charles prorogued parliament (suspended its sitting). In August 1628 Buckingham was assassinated, but this did nothing to solve the underlying problems. Charles was furious at the attitude of parliament, whom he regarded as irresponsible and reluctant to contribute to the needs of the government, and he was both unable and unwilling to accept the need to account for his policies in the way that MPs wished. Although the parliament of 1628 did grant subsidies, he regarded their demand for accountability on the part of ministers, if not of the king himself, as too high a price to pay.

When MPs' complaints were renewed in the next parliamentary session in 1629, the king decided to end such fruitless arguments by proroguing parliament once more. However, when his message reached the Commons, angry MPs held the Speaker in his chair to prevent their dismissal while they passed Three Resolutions. In this act of open defiance they expressed their grievances over arbitrary imprisonment, the collection of taxes without parliamentary consent, and the changes being introduced in the Church. Charles favoured the minority, Arminian wing of Anglicans, who wished to restore traditional ceremonies and increase the authority of bishops in the Church. In 1626 he had appointed one of this group, William Laud, as Bishop of London, and in 1633 he became Archbishop of Canterbury. Under Laud's leadership new ceremonies were introduced, altars removed to the east end of churches and railed off from the laity, preaching discouraged in favour of set prayers, and rules, old and new, rigidly enforced. Puritans who, up to then, had got by with a token acceptance were now forced to obey or leave. Essentially, the practical compromise with puritan feeling that had been operated by both Elizabeth and James was shattered.

To make matters worse, these policies were conducted against a background of growing leniency towards Catholics. Recusancy laws which fined Catholics for not attending Church were enforced, possibly for the income that they produced, but under the patronage of the queen a Catholic party developed at Court (for example the Catholic Lord Weston was Lord Treasurer until his death in 1635), and in 1637 an envoy from the pope was publicly received and honoured by the king. Complaints against such policies led to harsh punishments - in 1637 three protesters, Burton, Bastwick and Prynne were publicly mutilated and imprisoned for writing and publishing attacks on the queen and on Laud's policies. All three had their ears clipped, and Prynne was also branded on the face. The event was particularly shocking to contemporaries, since such brutal punishments were not normally applied to the gentry or professional classes except in extreme cases.

The other significant appointment made by Charles at this time was that of Sir Thomas Wentworth, who was created Lord Strafford and a member of the Privy Council in 1628. Strafford had participated in the attacks on Buckingham in the 1620s, and his acceptance of office (he became Lord President of the Council of the North in 1628 and Lord Deputy of Ireland in 1632) was regarded by many MPs as a betrayal. Strafford's complaints, however, had been motivated mainly by Buckingham's inefficiency, and this concern for efficient government characterised his work in both the North of England and in Ireland. The hand of central government was increasingly felt in the localities, more especially because of Charles's attempts to raise new revenue and secure financial independence from parliament. Monopolies were sold again and forest laws and feudal payments were revived. But above all it was the levying of Ship Money that brought the government close to success. This was an ancient and occasional tax, levied on ports and coastal towns to pay for naval defence. Charles levied the tax in 1634, and in 1635 extended it to inland areas. By 1636 it was clearly becoming a regular tax and was being used for a wider range of government expenses. Challenged in the courts by John Hampden in 1637, it was declared legal although the judges were divided in their opinions. This was a serious blow to those who hoped to use parliament and the king's financial needs to restrain Charles, and in 1637-8 both John Pym and the Duke of Bedford, leaders of the puritan faction, were considering emigration as a way out.

2 The Road To War

What changed the situation was the ill-fated attempt in 1637 to impose a revised English Prayer Book on the Church in Scotland. Charles was determined to create uniformity of government, and in particular of religion, in the three kingdoms (England/Wales, Ireland and Scotland) which he ruled as separate units. This was not unreasonable, and James had already taken steps in that direction. The English parliament had rejected his plans for Anglo-Scottish union in 1607, but he had encouraged Protestant settlement by both Scots and English in Ireland. By 1621 he had persuaded the Scots to accept bishops in the Scottish Church, but in the face of widespread opposition to further change, he had the sense to slow down. By nature and conviction, however, Charles lacked such caution. In 1637 the use of the Prayer Book in St. Giles Cathedral in Edinburgh sparked off a riot which turned to a widespread rebellion known, appropriately, as the Bishops' Wars. In 1638 a Scottish assembly rejected both the prayer book and the bishops, and a National Covenant (agreement) was set up to defend the Presbyterian system. The Covenanters raised an army which defeated Charles in 1639 and forced him to sign the Treaty of Berwick. This allowed a Scottish synod (assembly of ministers) to decide on the organisation of the Church. They confirmed the decisions of 1638, rejecting the Prayer Book and abolishing bishops. This made Charles determined to crush the rebellion. In April 1640 he called parliament, believing that traditional anti-Scottish feeling would rally sufficient support to gain supplies, but the opposition leaders were already in touch with the Scots, and insisted that their grievances be considered first. Charles angrily dismissed MPs (creating the nickname of the Short Parliament) and published new Canons (rules) for the Church, which embodied and enforced the changes made by Laud. At this point the Scots invaded England and besieged Newcastle. Charles called a Great Council of the nobility to meet at York, but his appeal for loans was met by the Twelve Peers Petition which requested him to call parliament. When the Scots insisted on a new truce (the Treaty of Ripon) in which Charles was committed to pay the costs of their army (£850 a day) it was clear that he no longer had any other option. On 3 November 1640 the parliament that was to be known as the Long Parliament assembled at Westminster.

The calling of the Long Parliament brought the crisis to a head, but it was not necessarily a prelude to war. In 1640, hopes of a settlement were high, and even Charles accepted that he would have to make some concessions. In February 1641 he reluctantly accepted the Triennial Act which guaranteed that parliament would meet at least once every three years. Proceedings had already begun for the impeachment of Strafford and Laud, by which they would face trial in the House of Lords, and by April it was clear that there was insufficient evidence to convict Strafford of treason. The opposition leaders rapidly substituted a Bill of Attainder, which, if passed by parliament, would simply declare him legally guilty. This required no trial but it did require the king's assent. To obtain this, Pym, who had emerged as the main leader of the opposition group in the House of Commons, raised the political temperature by revealing a plot by the king's more extreme supporters to dissolve parliament by force (the first army plot) and then by using public demonstrations intimidated the king into signing Strafford's death warrant. In May 1641 Strafford was executed, and an act passed to prevent the dissolution of Parliament without its consent. This was followed by a series of measures which declared non-parliamentary taxation, and Ship Money in particular, to be illegal, and abolished instruments of royal power such as the Prerogative Courts of Star Chamber, the High Commission and the regional Councils of the North and the Marches (the Welsh borderlands). The purpose of this was to secure the independence of local government and reduce the effectiveness of central control as it had been exercised under the supervision of Strafford and Laud.

However, by the early summer of 1641 problems were beginning to arise in the opposition campaign. In May the Commons had passed a Bill to exclude Bishops from the House of Lords, but in June this was rejected by the Upper House. In the same month, the Root and Branch Bill, which abolished bishops in the Church, had to be laid aside after debate, since it clearly would not pass the Commons. The Ten Propositions which were presented to the king, claiming the right for parliament to approve his choice of advisers, were disliked by a significant minority of MPs as encroaching on the king's legitimate powers. In August 1641 the king visited Scotland, amid opposition fears that he would negotiate a peace which would leave him free to dissolve parliament by force. It was clear that many MPs felt that their task was complete and that the opposition leaders were pushing too far, to the point of altering the balance of the constitution. It was equally clear that a party which could be termed Royalist in its sympathy for the king and the Anglican Church was beginning to emerge.

These concerns were swept aside in October/November 1641 as news came of a far worse horror across the water - the outbreak of a Catholic Rebellion in Ireland. It was clear that an army would be needed to deal with this, and the king requested money for such a force when he returned to London in November. The problem for the opposition was that, while they desired to rescue Ireland, they dared not place an army in the hands of a king whom they distrusted. Accordingly, they sought to attach a condition to the Militia Bill which would enable parliament to control the choice of army commander. Not only did they thus insult the king, but they launched an overt appeal for political support in the Grand Remonstrance of November/December, which was introduced in parliament and then published. Such an unprecedented public appeal infuriated the more cautious MPs, who regarded it as an insult to the king and an incitement to public disorder. Sensing that support was moving his way and eager to seize the opportunity, the king entered the House of Commons in early January in order to arrest Five Members whom he considered to be the opposition leaders, only to find that they had been warned in time to escape.

Success in arresting the Five Members might have paid off, but failure was disastrous. Waverers were convinced of the king's willingness to resort to violence and MPs were infuriated by the assault on their privileges. With mobs demonstrating in the city, the King left London on 9 January. He went to York where many of his supporters joined him. In their absence Pym was able to turn the Militia Bill into a parliamentary Militia Ordinance, which did not require the king's consent. It was passed in March 1642. In April the king tried to strengthen his position by taking control of the substantial arsenal of weapons kept at Hull, but was refused entry by the parliamentary Governor, Sir John Hotham. Charles declared Hotham a traitor, and there followed a propaganda battle between king and parliament. In June an apparent attempt at negotiation was initiated by parliament in the Nineteen Propositions but their demands were too extreme to make a peaceful outcome realistic. In August the king made the final, decisive move when he raised his standard at Nottingham and called for volunteers.

3 From Civil War to Republic

War proceeded slowly at first, in a series of local skirmishes, as each side manoeuvred to gain the advantage. In October 1642 the battle of Edgehill ended in stalemate, but the king's road to London lay open until the royalist army was held up by the volunteers of the London trained bands at Turnham Green. The king withdrew to Oxford while two of his supporters, the Earl of Newcastle and Sir Ralph Hopton, secured most of the north and the south-west for him. In 1643, after the failure of peace talks in the Oxford Negotiations, the royalists attempted a three-pronged advance on London, but were held up by the resistance of Hull, Plymouth and Gloucester. In an effort to break the military deadlock John Pym negotiated an alliance with the Scottish Covenanters. In October this was enshrined in the Solemn League and Covenant by which parliament committed itself to the establishment of a Presbyterian Church in return for the help of a Scottish army. In December, Pym died, but the value of the alliance was demonstrated in July 1644 when the Scots helped to defeat the royalists at Marston Moor, securing control of the north of England for parliament. However, this success was negated by the failure of the parliamentary general, the Earl of Essex, in the south-west, where he was forced to surrender an army of over 6,000 men. This fuelled the frustration of the more radical party in parliament who wanted a unified command and a more vigorous prosecution of the war. These demands came to a head in the Self-denying Ordinance of April 1645, by which it was agreed that no member of parliament (including members of the House of Lords) could hold a military command. This effectively excluded the inadequate aristocratic leadership of Essex and Manchester, and prepared the way for the establishment of the New Model Army with Sir Thomas Fairfax as General and Oliver Cromwell as his second-in-command.

The establishment of a single, disciplined army, led by men of military talent, represented a much more efficient use of resources and provided a mobile and effective fighting force. Its value was first demonstrated in the defeat of the main royalist army at Naseby in June 1645, after which it efficiently mopped up the remaining royalist resistance. In June 1646 came the surrender of Oxford, the king having already surrendered himself to the Scots in May. By the end of 1646 he was in the hands of parliament, which appeared to have fulfilled its aims.

However, military success was to prove more easily attainable than political settlement. Already differences had emerged on the parliamentary side between those who supported the establishment of a Presbyterian national Church, and those (known as Independents) who wanted to allow some freedom for groups of (Protestant) separatists to establish their own, voluntary congregations. In 1644-5 this dispute had wrecked the work of the Assembly of Divines which had been set up to arrange reform of the Church. By 1646 conservatives were complaining bitterly of the radicalism encouraged and protected in the New Model Army, with soldiers preaching and, according to Richard Baxter, 'arguing for Church, and sometimes state, democracy'. In London the campaign for religious toleration had taken an even more dangerous turn, with the emergence of a Leveller Movement which demanded religious liberty as a natural right for all, coupled with the reform of parliament and the establishment of a genuinely representative, parliamentary republic. The response of the conservative majority in parliament was to hasten a settlement with the king and the disbandment of the New Model Army. This was ordered early in 1647, without settling the soldiers' arrears of pay or ensuring that they would be indemnified for their actions during the war. Army protests were dismissed, leaving no doubt that its civil and religious concerns would receive short shrift once disbandment took place. The effect was to politicise the army under the leadership of Cromwell and his son-in-law, Henry Ireton. They attempted to establish a settlement by negotiating with the king, but unfortunately Charles saw these events as an opportunity to play off his enemies against one another. While Cromwell and Ireton struggled to contain Leveller influence in the army at the Putney Debates of October/November 1647, the king continued to play for time, pretending to consider both the army proposals (the Heads of the Proposals) and parliament's Newcastle Propositions. In fact he was secretly negotiating to renew the war. In the spring of 1648 royalist risings broke out in Wales and the south-east, and a Scottish army invaded England in support of the king, who had promised a temporary establishment of Presbyterianism in the Church.

Faced with this betrayal, the army and parliament now united to win this Second Civil War. The risings were quickly crushed, and the Scots were defeated at Preston. More importantly, the army now regarded Charles as a 'man of blood', responsible for the death and destruction of war, rejected by God and guilty of treason. In November 1648 an army remonstrance written by Ireton called for his trial and execution, and when the parliamentary conservatives attempted to re-open negotiations with Charles in December the regiment of Colonel Pride was sent to forcibly exclude them from the House of Commons. Pride's Purge of 6 December 1648 opened the way to the trial of the king, as the remaining 'Rump' of MPs set up a court and sat in judgement upon him. The verdict and sentence were a foregone conclusion. On 30 January 1649 Charles I was beheaded at Whitehall, and three months later the monarchy and House of Lords were abolished in favour of a parliamentary republic.

4 Postscript - from Republic to Restoration

Charles I's eldest son returned to England amid joyous celebrations in May 1660. The monarchy was restored and the reign of Charles II began. It is therefore self-evident that this republic did not last long. Strictly speaking, it was removed in 1653 when the Protectorate government of Oliver Cromwell was established. However, the inability of those who executed Charles to establish a stable régime to replace him should not be allowed to disguise the significance of what happened in 1649 - at that point the Restoration was not a foregone conclusion. If there ever was an 'English Revolution', it surely occurred in 1649, and if it was a revolution that ultimately failed, it has not been without significance in the development of English, and British, government and society.

Making use of the 'Outline of Events'

The outline above can serve both as a general introduction to the period and as a point of reference to which you can return as you work through later chapters. At this stage it is important that you make yourself familiar with the broad outline of events and the main developments arising from them. The best way is to try to use the material to establish a general picture of what happened and why. To achieve this you may find it useful to carry out one or more of the exercises suggested below.

1. Re-read sections 1) and 2) and draw up a list of causes of the outbreak of Civil War. Divide them into conditional causes (those which made it possible or probable that war would occur) and contingent causes (those which made war happen at the time and in the way it did). At what point did war become inevitable?

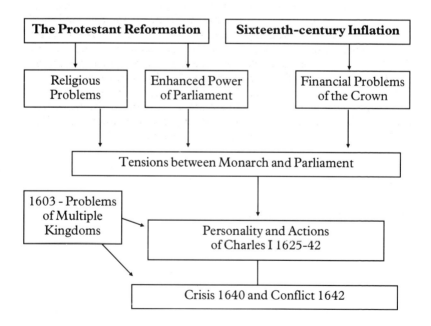

Summary - Introduction

2. On a single sheet of A4 paper for each one, draw up a timeline of events which explain
    a) the outbreak of war, and,
    b) the execution of Charles I.
    The value of this exercise is that you will not be able to include all the relevant events, and you will therefore have to select those that you consider to have been most important. You can then compare your selection with those made by others, and discuss the reasons for your choice. It does not matter if you find it difficult to make a selection at this stage - there is no 'right' answer, and the process of thinking and discussing will help you to develop your ideas.
3. Given that there was a restoration of the monarchy in 1660, historians disagree about how far the events of 1640-9 can be called an 'English Revolution'. To form an initial view of your own, draw up a list of the characteristics that you associate with 'revolution' and summarise how far the events of 1640-9 meet these requirements. You can then compare and consider your ideas alongside those of others.

CHAPTER 2

Interpretations of the Civil Wars

The purpose of this chapter is to provide the reader with an understanding of the historical context in which the Civil Wars took place, and to establish some preliminary ideas and hypotheses about their nature and significance. This will be done by examining and evaluating different interpretations put forward by historians who have studied the period.

1 History, Politics, and the Civil Wars

'The Civil War', wrote the historian Ronald Hutton,'has raged on paper ever since the blood stopped flowing'. This is a view supported by C.V.Wedgewood in *The King's Peace* (1955) when she stated that, 'the final, dispassionate, authoritative history of the Civil Wars cannot be written until the problems have ceased to matter; by that time it will not be worth writing'. It is certainly likely that, if one could quantify the matter, more ink has been expended on the Civil Wars of the seventeenth century than on any other single issue in British history. Nor has the pace and intensity of debate shown any signs of lessening in recent years. Historians continue to disagree on the causes, nature and significance of events without any sign of reaching a consensus regarding what has become known as 'The English Revolution'.

The reasons for this lie partly in the nature of history itself. This has been defined by E.H. Carr as, 'an unending dialogue between the present and the past' – in which the concerns and preoccupations of different generations of historians lead them to emphasise new issues as well as to reinterpret the old. The point was elaborated by the Dutch historian Pieter Geyl (1887-1966) in his *Napoleon: For and Against* (1949).

1 The lack of finality [he wrote of interpretations of Napoleon] strikes me as both unavoidable and natural ... As soon as there is a question of explanation, of interpretation, of appreciation, though the special method of the historian [the need for evidence] remains
5 valuable, the personal element can no longer be ruled out ... Every historical narrative is dependent upon explanation, interpretation, appreciation. In other words, we cannot see the past in a single, communicable picture except from a point of view, which implies a choice, a personal perspective. It is impossible that two historians
10 living in different periods, should see any historical personality in the same light. The greater the political importance of an historical character [or issue] the more impossible this is.

Geyl's comments apply to any historical issue, but the reasons for the peculiar fascination of the Civil Wars are indicated in his final sentence. The political importance of any such event - bitter, harsh and by nature divisive - is bound to be great, but this is particularly true when the issues over which it was fought remain unresolved, as was the case in 1660. The political problems which divided men in 1642 and in 1649 set the agenda for political development in the following centuries and the Civil War became part of a living political tradition. Eighteenth-century Whigs and nineteenth-century reformers drew on ideas first expressed in the Civil War period in their arguments for parliamentary government and political reform. Conservatives of all kinds pointed out its dangers and argued that gradual, evolutionary change, was preferable to the risk of upheaval. Modern-day radicals revived the ideas and reputations of the radical minority who flourished in the hot-house conditions of war and religious freedom. Thus the political divisions of the eighteenth and nineteenth centuries, the battle for parliamentary power and later for parliamentary reform, involved issues to which the Civil War remained directly relevant.

By the end of the nineteenth century, with liberal, parliamentary forces triumphant, the orthodox historical interpretation of the Civil Wars was that of the Whigs, in whose view they formed a part of the longer struggle for parliamentary government. In the twentieth century, however, this comfortable consensus was destroyed as the Civil Wars were re-examined from a new political standpoint. This standpoint was labelled 'Marxist' (largely by opponents) since it drew on the historical analysis by which Karl Marx justified and predicted the eventual political victory of socialism. On this basis, Marxist historians came to see the Civil Wars as the 'English Revolution', equated with bourgeois (middle-class) revolutions in France in 1789 and in Russia in February 1917. They also saw strong elements of class conflict in the failed attempts of more radical groups to take the 'revolution' further in 1647-9. Thus the Marxist historians offered a challenge, not only to existing views of the nature and significance of the Civil Wars, but also to existing assumptions about the British political system, its acceptability and its future development. Once more, the causes, nature and significance of the Civil Wars had become relevant to living political issues and an on-going political debate. In time, Marxist interpretations were successfully challenged in terms of their historical validity, on the basis of historical evidence, and necessary revisions were made which are examined in more detail further on. In some cases, however, the challenge has been associated with contemporary political perspectives and a continuing attack on socialist ideas.

Those whose political purpose has been to discredit, not only Marxist history, but also the intellectual validity of Marxism itself, have created a new historical 'school' seeking to challenge both liberal and socialist assumptions about the past. In particular, historians of the political 'right' have tended to dismiss any idea of a seventeenth-century 'English

Revolution' and to challenge the inspiration drawn from the period by the political 'left' of all kinds. One example of such work is Jonathan Clark's *Revolution and Rebellion* (1986) described by R.C. Richardson in a recent historiographical survey as both 'Thatcherite' and 'deliberately provocative'. Thus the capacity of this crucial era to generate political heat remains as strong as ever.

The continuation and development of these debates can be traced through the historiography of the Civil Wars, as each generation has approached the subject in terms of its own political divisions and has sought to reinterpret the views of the past. The result has been a process of continual conflict which has also produced a growing accumulation of knowledge. While reinterpretation necessarily focusses on what is different, each generation has nevertheless absorbed and accepted large areas of knowledge from its predecessors. Thus the study of history is a cumulative process, in which new understandings can eventually be added to the old to create a synthesis rather than a replacement. In the Bibliography attached to his *Century of Revolution,* the 'Marxist' historian Christopher Hill directs the serious student to the work of the great 'Whig' historian, S.R. Gardiner, whose political and constitutional interpretation of the Civil War he was seeking to challenge. Gardiner's work, he implies, continues to be valuable, on its own merits and because it can be read and interpreted in the light of later research.

What this means in practice is that any study of the Civil Wars benefits from an introductory context which considers the different interpretations put forward by those who have studied them in the past. In these interpretations, historians have sought to explain the causes of the wars as well as the events within them, since the issues that caused war have implications for what that war meant, and how its significance should be interpreted. If, for example, the Civil Wars are seen to have been caused by deep-seated problems within seventeenth-century society or its system of government, it is more likely that they will be viewed as having genuinely revolutionary significance than if they arose merely from the mistakes of Charles I or the personal ambitions of his opponents. An exhaustive survey is not possible here, but by summarising the contribution made by different 'schools' of historians the remainder of this chapter seeks to provide both an historical context in which the seventeenth-century problems that led up to the Civil Wars can be introduced, and a historiographical context, raising issues for debate. Ultimately, the student must consider the evidence and the events for him or herself, in order to evaluate the different interpretations that have been offered, and to draw conclusions about the issues concerned. What is provided further on is intended as a starting point.

2 Early Interpretations of the Civil Wars

From the outset, accounts of the Civil War and its causes have been influenced by the political views of their authors. For Lord Clarendon, who as Edward Hyde was the leader of a moderate royalist group in the Long Parliament and who later became chief adviser to Charles II, the war was a Great Rebellion fomented by the ambition of the king's opponents. On the other hand, Thomas May (1595-1650) who was one of the Long Parliament's secretaries, wrote two accounts - the *History of the Parliament of England* (1647) and *A Breviary of the History of the Parliament of England* (1650) - in which the blame for both the outbreak of war and the abolition of the monarchy was laid firmly at the door of Charles I. These accounts set the tone for those that followed. With the emergence of the Whig party in the struggle to exclude James II from power, and their victory in the Glorious Revolution of 1688-9, the parliamentarian viewpoint began to take precedence, and a Whig interpretation of history began to take shape. In this view the Civil War was part of a struggle for political liberty and the Protestant religion against the attempt by Charles I and his sons to establish absolute monarchy and a Catholic tyranny. Although this interpretation did not go completely unchallenged, by the nineteenth century it had become an established orthodoxy which could be applied by contemporaries in different ways. For most, like the historian and nineteenth-century politician, Thomas Babington Macaulay, it formed the basis on which to demonstrate the virtues of parliamentary government as developed in Britain and America.

All these interpretations unashamedly drew on history as part of contemporary political struggles. Macaulay, for example, made no attempt at a balanced interpretation of characters or events, and was content to portray James II as nothing less than a Catholic tyrant. However, the nineteenth-century development of scientific study, with its rules of evidence and experimental proof, and the spread of education and new educational institutions created a generation of historians, often professional academics, who took pride in 'scientific' methods and professional objectivity. Claiming to avoid political standpoints and to base their conclusions on the objective study of documentary evidence, historians such as S.R. Gardiner in his *History of England, 1603-56* (1883-4) provided the first modern historical accounts of the Civil War as well as the model and methodology upon which modern historical study is based. What they did not provide, however, was a radically new interpretation of the Civil War. In the words of R.C. Richardson in his *The Debate on the English Revolution Revisited* (1991), 'Scientific history did not destroy the Whig interpretation of history; it merely diluted it'. Gardiner and his colleagues might attempt to establish a balanced view, but they could not escape from their own perceptions of good and evil and their Victorian liberal upbringing. This had given them a Whig view of 'progress' in which they perceived history as the story of the development of political liberty from primitive society to the pinnacle of late nineteenth-century Britain.

3 The 'Standard' Whig Interpretation

The result was that the 'standard' Whig interpretation provided an explanation of the Civil War based above all on political and religious issues, as reflected in the preferred epithet of 'Puritan Revolution'. The protagonists were judged mainly on the extent to which they contributed to the development of political and religious 'progress'. The origins of the struggle were seen to lie in the development of the English Protestantism after the Reformation and the Elizabethan settlement of 1559. The Protestant religion was said to have encouraged greater individual thought and a desire for political and intellectual liberty which increasingly found its spokesmen in parliament and in particular in the House of Commons. Hence the Puritan movement, as the most comprehensively Protestant group, were in the vanguard of the struggle. Their main purpose was to purify the Anglican Church of the remaining traces of popery (Catholic practices) and since the queen refused to consider reform and the bishops enforced the existing rules, they tried to introduce change through parliament. In 1570 Thomas Cartwright, a Cambridge scholar, put forward a scheme of Presbyterian organisation, similar to that in Scotland, in which a simplified and purified church would be run at a parish level by ministers and lay Elders, and at a national level through a series of representative committees, or synods. In 1571 and again in 1587, attempts were made to introduce bills into the House of Commons to establish elements of this system, which were promptly forbidden by the queen. These attempts to use parliament in the cause of religious reform, combined with anti-Catholic concerns over the queen's marriage (or lack of it) and her cautious foreign policy, led to a growing awareness of parliamentary rights and to tension with a monarch who sought to restrict debate. Tension was contained in the reign of Elizabeth by her enormous political authority and the skill with which she played upon parliamentary loyalties, but the accession of the extravagant and tactless James I, with his high-flown claims of Divine Right, led to a marked deterioration. James's perceptions of the Divine Right of Kings led him to emphasise that, receiving his royal power from God, he was responsible only to God, and in theory, above any earthly law. In practice he was more cautious, but his claims raised parliamentary fears.

By the time Charles I came to the throne in 1625 the political situation was already ominous. MPs' refusal to grant Charles tunnage and poundage for life showed their suspicion of his character and their desire to use finance as a means of maintaining parliamentary influence. Charles, however, refused to accept any restrictions. Believing in his

Divine Right he continued to collect tunnage and poundage and to raise money by other dubious methods such as forced loans. In 1628 the Commons protested in the Petition of Right, which the king accepted in order to obtain a parliamentary grant of taxes, and then ignored. This tyranny was made worse by his religious policies. Not content, like his predecessors, with merely restraining Puritan activity in the Church, he adopted High Church Arminian policies. This involved increasing the level of ceremonies and set prayers, reducing the importance of preaching and Bible study (both of which were seen by puritans as essential) and raising the authority of the bishops in a way that resembled Catholicism. To make matters worse, Charles also married a French Catholic princess, Henrietta Maria, allowed her brother to suppress a French Protestant rebellion, and permitted her openly to practise the Catholic religion. After further parliamentary protests in 1629 he decided to assert his authority once and for all, by dispensing with parliament entirely. In the ensuing Eleven Years Tyranny he tried to establish efficient government on the model of continental absolutism, aided by Sir Thomas Wentworth (later Lord Strafford) and the Arminian, William Laud who became Archbishop of Canterbury in 1633. Although Charles himself was not a Catholic, his devotion to High Church views as well as his French wife allowed Catholic influence to creep in. Only when he overreached himself by trying to enforce his religious views on the Presbyterian Scots in 1637-40 was he forced by lack of money to recall parliament.

Supporters of the Puritan Revolution theory therefore identified political and religious changes, and the ambitions of Charles I as the main causes of the Civil War. Given Charles's character, no compromise settlement was possible, either in 1640-2 or in 1648-9. Moreover, the stresses and strains of war in itself had changed the situation by the later date. The need to win the struggle led to moderate leaders being replaced by the more committed parliamentarians, often with strong religious views. Some at least were Independents, believing in the right of individual congregations of 'Saints' to separate from the national Church and set up independent meetings. Under the leadership of a minority of 'Saints' like Oliver Cromwell, the New Model Army was formed to win the war. It also became a hotbed of religious and political extremism in which new ideas of religious toleration and political revolution began to take shape. The clumsy attempt of parliamentary leaders to get rid of it in 1647 led to a new 'revolution' in which the army seized the king as a bargaining counter in their struggle for religious liberty and arrears of pay. Cromwell and other officers who shared the army's religious concerns but not their political views were forced to place themselves at the head of this movement, in order to preserve army unity and exercise some measure of influence.

Charles saw an opportunity to divide his enemies by pretending to negotiate with both parliament and army, while secretly arranging help from Scotland. In 1648 this led to a Second Civil War in which he was easily defeated and which sealed his fate. Cromwell and the leading officers, who had previously sought to control the more radical elements of the army, were now convinced that Charles could not be trusted and that his refusal to compromise was a sign from God that he should be punished as a 'man of blood'. The result was a purge of parliament to remove the more conservative element (Pride's Purge in December 1648), and the king's trial and execution. A few months later the enforced abolition of the monarchy saw the establishment of republican government, but with only minority support the new government was dependent on the army. Through a series of failed constitutional experiments the régime was held together by the authority and determination of Oliver Cromwell, who struggled vainly to establish a moderate constitutional settlement and a measure of religious freedom. With his death in 1658 the strength of the régime collapsed, the morale of the army disintegrated, and the monarchy was restored by parliament in the belief that Charles II would govern constitutionally. This proved not to be entirely the case and the unresolved struggle for liberty continued thereafter until James II fled in 1688 after failing to establish absolute monarchy and the Catholic religion.

This account, simplified as it is, summarises the main features that concerned Gardiner, and also those of the next generations who pursued historical research into the Civil Wars, such as G.M.Trevelyan. This did not mean that they were in total agreement. The relative importance of different personalities, the nature of religious views and conflicts, the motivation of individuals and a range of other issues were open to interpretation, and hence to debate. In particular, radical ideas were examined and admired as a truly revolutionary feature of the period, or characterised as dangerous excesses creating a conservative backlash that destroyed the positive achievements of moderate reformers. Much valuable research was carried out, and many features of the above summary remain valid as partial explanations of what was happening in seventeenth-century England. What all such explanations shared, however, and what ultimately limited their authority, were two characteristics. The first was that they viewed the struggle from the standpoint that political 'progress' was encompassed within an Anglo-American version of parliamentary democracy, and judged historical events from that perspective. The second was that their scope was entirely limited to issues of politics and religion. It was this perception that was to be challenged by a new 'school' of historians influenced by the work of social scientists such as Max Weber, the Christian Socialist ideas of R.H.Tawney, and ultimately the materialist views of Karl Marx.

4 The 'Marxist' School

The term 'Marxist' has been used (rather loosely and often by political opponents) to describe a number of historians who challenged the Whig concentration on political history by arguing that political events were largely determined by the underlying economic developments which shaped society. In socialist theory, historical development has been shaped by the transition from a feudal economy based on land to a bourgeois capitalism based on trade, commerce and industrial production, and will in time be transformed into a socialist economy based on ownership of these assets by the population as a whole. Marx argued that the exploitation of land by a feudal aristocracy led *inevitably* to the development of a market economy and therefore a bourgeois commercial class, and that in time, this bourgeoisie would seek to acquire the political power that its wealth and importance merited. In Marxist terms the English 'gentry' who exploited their estates commercially were part of the bourgeoisie rather than the feudal nobility, and the Civil War represented the bid for power by a gentry-merchant House of Commons against the king and nobility who barred their way.

These ideas were first applied to English (or British) history in the work of R.H. Tawney, who built on the ideas put forward in Max Weber's *The Protestant Ethic and the Spirit of Capitalism* (1904). In 1926 Tawney published his major work, *Religion and the Rise of Capitalism,* in which he argued that Protestantism, and in particular the Puritan form with its emphasis on individual effort and success as proof of God's approval, provided the rising bourgeoisie with the ideal justification for their growing wealth and a bid for a greater share in power. He also pointed out that at least one contemporary commentator on the seventeenth-century conflict, James Harrington, had seen the connection between changes in the distribution of wealth and upheaval in the political system.

Tawney's legacy was taken up by a number of historians, but in particular by Christopher Hill. In his earliest work Hill interpreted the Civil War as the crucial turning-point in the bourgeois seizure of power. His views were more fully developed in *The Century of Revolution* (1961) where he argued that the rising gentry and their merchant allies had benefited from growing trade and sought to develop their estates by capitalist methods. They were frustrated by the barriers to commercial development that were created by a feudal monarchy which treated the national economy first and foremost as a source of wealth for the king. Particular grievances were the granting of monopolies which restricted trade and raised prices, rising customs duties, and the failure to protect trade against pirate attacks or rivals such as the Dutch. In the light of this last complaint, Charles's use of Ship Money to finance his régime in the 1630s was particularly galling. Fortified by a puritan conviction that

God approved their cause, this gentry-merchant alliance launched an assault on royal power through their growing control of parliament and the king's financial needs. This would inevitably produce a conflict of some kind, although its precise form and timing depended upon the activities of individuals and thus the advent of war *in 1642* resulted from the inept handling of the situation by Charles I. Nevertheless, the Civil War was essentially the result of underlying socio-economic forces, and the role of religion was to provide an ideology through which these underlying forces could be expressed.

This process continued after the outbreak of war, with the emergence of more radical groups such as the Levellers. Although their initial inspiration was religious and their ideas were formed in the separatist puritan groups of 'saints', they also represented an element of class conflict which took them beyond religion towards social revolution. For a brief period in 1647-49 their influence in the New Model Army brought them close to success. However, faced with this threat of popular revolution from below, the governing class closed ranks and eventually brought about the Restoration of the monarchy as a guarantee of their power. That monarchy was, however, permanently changed. Its feudal rights were not restored, and its power rested on an alliance with bourgeois capitalism, symbolised by the Navigation Acts, which protected British merchants from foreign competition, and the development of parliamentary government after 1660.

The work of Tawney and Hill set the agenda for a generation of historians. On the one hand, there were many who found their ideas plausible. The links between puritanism and commercial success seemed to be well-documented, and the tendency for towns and trading corporations to support parliament in the struggle reinforced the argument. At first sight the division of England into a royalist north and west and a more economically advanced, parliamentarian south-east fitted the patterns of allegiance at the outbreak of war. There is a great deal of evidence to link a puritan 'middling-sort' of yeomen and craftsmen with parliamentary activity and later with radical ideas.

On the other hand, almost every aspect of Hill's argument has been seriously challenged. In particular, the idea that there was an equation between support for parliament and 'rising' gentry was strongly attacked, notably by Hugh Trevor-Roper. He found a significant correlation between support for parliament and the lesser or 'mere' gentry who lacked influence at Court and were forced to rely on their income from land in a period of rising prices. He concluded that, far from representing a revolt of forward-thinking, economically advanced members of the political élite against a backward looking feudal régime, the Civil War was an attempt by a declining gentry to halt the erosion of their power by a dynamic, centralising and overbearing Court. It was the king who encouraged economic development and exploitation in schemes such as fen drainage, and whose increasing use of the Privy

Council and the Prerogative Courts was threatening the position of the 'mere' gentry in the localities. This view has in turn been subjected to detailed analysis and scrutiny. It has been found to be more convincing, in social and economic terms, when applied to those who supported the revolution of 1649 (the execution of the king and abolition of monarchy) than to those who supported parliament in 1642. Even then, it represents only a partial explanation of the beliefs and motivations of the revolutionaries.

The 'Marxist' interpretation of the Civil War, labelling it the 'English Revolution' to equate with those in France and Russia, has been challenged at every level, and few would defend it wholesale. Christopher Hill himself has revised his earlier interpretations to accommodate a more sophisticated understanding of historical relationships. In particular, he has argued that the nature of the Civil War as an economic and political turning-point does not depend upon its having been consciously planned as such - that it is the results, rather than the intentions of participants, that determine the significance of such events. Along with other 'Marxist' historians such as A.L. Morton and H.N. Brailsford, he also explored more fully the 'revolution within the revolution' pursued by radical groups such as the Levellers, Ranters and Diggers, who sought to reform society as well as politics. Hill came to the conclusion that while these groups were less clearly defined and organised than has sometimes been claimed, they did represent an important and enduring element of radicalism within English society, whose ideals and aspirations have been suppressed and disguised by official restraints and censorship. Again, these views have been challenged on both historical and political grounds. It has been argued that Hill has over-estimated both the influence and the revolutionary ideology of the radicals, thereby inflating the Civil Wars into the revolution that, in his opponents' eyes, England never had.

Despite the fact that significant parts of their interpretation have been successfully called into question, the contribution of Marxist ideas to the debate on the Civil War has been immeasurable. In the first place, they have broken the monopoly of religion and politics. Whatever part these factors played (and it is undoubtedly important) they must now be set against a view of society as a whole, and account must be taken of a dimension that the Whig interpretation ignored. Secondly, they have opened the way to other major developments in historical explanation of the Civil War. Further investigation of aspects and issues raised by Marxist historians has produced much new work, including the increasing importance of local studies, and the work of the so-called 'revisionists'. In different ways these recent interpretations represent a reaction against the thematic, single-issue explanations offered by the Marxists and many of their opponents. Thus historians have sought to investigate particular aspects of the period in greater depth and to emphasise the varied and individual responses of many of those who participated in events. This has resulted in greater awareness of the complexity of reactions in seventeenth-century society, and a revival of interest in the political and religious issues which concerned the Whigs. Nevertheless, the legacy of Marxist ideas remains important, in that politics and religion are both now examined and assessed in the context of social development and the social structures that influenced them.

5 Recent Interpretations of the Civil War

The Civil War has always provided fertile ground for local history. In the nineteenth century numerous amateur historians sought to present a picture of how national events had been reflected in their own localities, and in the process, did much valuable work in collecting and preserving documentary sources which might otherwise have been lost. Many local studies were valuable and interesting in themselves, enriching the picture of national divisions and issues with a local dimension. In recent years, however, a different approach has been adopted. In the first place, the kind of generalisations made by 'Whigs' and 'Marxists' about the motivations of participants or the state of economic and social development seemed to require a testing and refinement for which local studies were ideal. Examples of such studies are J.T. Cliffe's *The Yorkshire Gentry from the Reformation to the Civil War* (1969) and H.A. Lloyd's *The Gentry of South-West Wales 1540-1640* (1968), both responding to the 'gentry controversy' described above. Studies of this kind continue to be produced and to be of value. A further development of local studies came with the work of Alan Everitt, especially in his *The Community of Kent and the Great Rebellion 1640-1660* (1966). Everitt refused to see local history as a miniature version of national events, and sought to study his subject on its own terms, as a local community which affected and was affected by events at the centre, but which filtered the relationship through its own preoccupations and perceptions. What he found was a county community of gentry whose response to the crisis and the war of 1642 was conditioned by its own local loyalties and the desire to protect its region. Thus his case study added a new dimension to our understanding of the Civil Wars by emphasising local interests and the extent to which they shaped, or took precedence over, the political and religious issues that were assumed to have divided and motivated participants.

Everitt's approach was taken further by Clive Holmes' study of *The Eastern Association* and John Morrill's work on Cheshire, both published in 1974, while Peter Clark's work on Kent (1977) and Ann Hughes' *Politics, Society and Civil War in Warwickshire 1620-1660* (1987) have challenged some of Everitt's conclusions while reinforcing his belief in the value of local history. Much of this historiographical development was summarised in John Morrill's *Revolt of the Provinces* (1976, 2nd edn. 1980) which, in the words of Dr R.C. Richardson, 'encapsulated many of the changing tendencies of post-Everitt writing on the local history of the English Revolution'. Dr Morrill traced the impact of the war on different localities, revealing widespread neutralism and reluctance to participate. He also showed clearly how local issues and considerations turned political and religious divisions into a rich and complex patchwork which destroys any attempt to comprehend the causes and impact of the Civil War within large-scale or one-dimensional generalisations. Significantly, he insists that it is not enough to examine the political and religious breakdown which occurred at the centre of affairs, and that the impact of such breakdown can only be understood in the context of economic and social structures at a local as well as at a national level.

A similar rejection of generalised explanations of the Civil War has characterised the work of many other historians who have sought to investigate aspects of the conflict in recent years. Detailed investigation of individual members of the Long Parliament was carried out by Brunton and Pennington in 1954, by David Underdown in *Pride's Purge* in 1971, and in Blair Worden's study of the Rump Parliament published in 1974. Close examination of different religious and political groups has characterised the work of J.H. Hexter, Mark Kishlansky, Conrad Russell and Nicholas Tyacke, in which traditional assumptions about the relationship between religious views and political loyalties have been both challenged and defended. Ronald Hutton has subjected the royalists to similar scrutiny, while Gerald Aylmer has carefully examined the nature of Civil War administration and the attitudes of those involved. Many historians have re-examined the role of the lower classes, sparking off a considerable debate. Brian Manning, Derek Hirst, Barry Reay, J.F. McGregor, William Lamont and David Underdown have all argued in their different ways that political activity among the lower classes was significant, although not by any means always sympathetic to parliament. The overall effect of this work has been to make the divisions within society and politics appear much less clear-cut and much more complex.

Such an approach, emphasising individual and particular factors rather than generalisations, has produced the so-called 'revisionist' school of historians who have argued that the Civil War was not the result of long-term structural changes, political or economic, but of the interaction of circumstances and personalities in the period immediately prior to its outbreak. Prominent within this group are Anthony Fletcher, whose study of *The Outbreak of the English Civil War* (1981) emphasises the unexpected and accidental nature of the conflict, and Conrad Russell, who has made a significant contribution to the historiography of the period by drawing attention to the 'British dimension'. This highlights the stresses and pressures upon government after 1603 which were created by the need to govern three separate and distinct kingdoms (England & Wales, Scotland, and Ireland), and shows how the interaction of factors and individuals across these kingdoms influenced the outcome of events at crucial times. His *Causes of the English Civil War* (1990) and *Fall of the British Monarchies* (1991) have offered a new synthesis of traditional and revisionist views. While stressing that the war was neither inevitable nor intended, he has shown how longer-term factors such as the monarchy's financial problems, religious divisions and 'the problem of multiple kingdoms' were brought to a head by Charles I. In his hands, problems relating to different parts of his three realms interacted to take matters beyond, not only his control, but also that of his opponents. This is a valuable interpretation, yet one which has already been subject to scrutiny and suggestions for improvement.

The outcome of recent historiography has therefore been twofold. In the first place, it has revived interest in, and debate about, political and religious issues, although awareness of the social and economic context is now accepted as an integral part of any valid judgement. An interesting new synthesis of political, social and economic explanations of the war has recently been offered by Jack Goldstone in his *Revolution and Rebellion in the Early Modern World* (1991). He attributes the breakdown of the social and political order to an underlying rise in population, which had both economic and social consequences and which posed problems with which the existing structure of government simply could not cope. Secondly, it has undermined belief that any single-issue explanation of the causes, nature or significance of the Civil War can ever be adequate. Few, if any, accepted generalisations remain intact. Even the assumption that the opposition was directed from an increasingly important House of Commons has been challenged by John Adamson's argument that the parliamentarian nobility played a leading role in the opposition campaign of 1640-2 and in the construction of the Heads of the Proposals (the army's proposed settlement) of 1647. Perhaps the only valid generalisation that can be made is that any published theories about the English Civil Wars will be subjected to intense and detailed analysis and to refinement if not challenges.

Those who would study the Civil Wars are left, therefore, with an embarrassment of riches. On the one hand, more is known and understood than ever before, and the possibilities for debate are both endless and fascinating. On the other hand, the very wealth of detailed research and awareness of the complexity of events makes comprehension difficult and generalisation dangerous. Nevertheless, generalisation of some kind is a necessary part of the study of history, because the 'facts' deduced from the evidence available have to be organised and managed if they are to form part of any coherent explanation. Any historian must, in the end, offer some over-arching generalisations which draw out the significance and emphasise the implications of the many individual points made. Thus Anthony Fletcher summarises his vastly detailed analysis of why war broke out by describing the development of 'competing myths' of tyranny and disorder, in which their warring creators eventually became trapped. Ann Hughes, in one of the best recent explorations of *The Causes of the English Civil War* (1991) suggests similarly competing 'conspiracy theories' set against a background of 'functional breakdown' (the breakdown of the governing system), in which the king was unable to govern according to traditional precepts. He was therefore forced to develop new measures which brought about resistance from a conservative governing class.

The significant point about many of the interpretations that have been summarised above, and those that have been excluded for lack of space, is the wide area of agreement that underlies the debate itself. Most historians agree that there were serious weaknesses in the system of government before 1640, and even before 1625. Most agree that Charles made serious errors in dealing with the situation and that he was not well-equipped in terms of character and self-confidence to perform well as a king. Most agree that the opposition leaders, called by Conrad Russell 'Pym's Junto', were far from revolutionary in their political outlook, although their religious views are a matter for greater debate. It is generally accepted that they too had their limitations, and that their errors also contributed to the outbreak of war. What tends to be at issue between different historians is often the precise mechanisms by which these factors interacted, the degree of responsibility to attribute to the two sides, and the relative importance of different factors and elements in the situation. Their views are influenced by personal and political interests, but also by the nature of the evidence itself, which is partial, often fragmentary and requires interpretation. Two things that students of history need, therefore, are an awareness of the limits of generalisation and a willingness to engage in on-going debate. The chapters which follow seek to facilitate this process by synthesising and summarising what is widely accepted, and by introducing areas for discussion. Ultimately the individual student must analyse and evaluate what is suggested, in order to develop his or her own judgements about the causes, nature and significance of the Civil Wars.

Making notes on 'Interpretations of the Civil War'

It is not expected that you will make detailed notes on the different interpretations described above. However, you may find it useful to briefly summarise the main points of some of them, in order to discuss and evaluate the ideas that they put forward. Task 1, below, is designed with this in mind.

1. Re-read and summarise:
    (a) the 'standard' Whig interpretation,
    (b) the Marxist interpretation,
    (c) the view put forward by Conrad Russell. Which of these interpretations do you find the most convincing? (Explain and justify your answer)

A good way of consolidating the understandings you have gained from this chapter and preparing yourself to tackle the next chapter would be to attempt the following three tasks.

2. What do you consider to be the value of local history in studying the Civil Wars?
3. Why is it possible for so many different interpretations of the Civil Wars to be put forward?
4. Use all the knowledge that you have acquired so far to put forward an explanation of the crisis in English government that emerged with the calling of the Long Parliament in 1640.

CHAPTER 3

From Crisis to Conflict, 1640-2

1 Introduction

The Civil War was an enormous shock and upheaval for those involved in it, and it is important not to underestimate the fear and horror with which such an event would be regarded. Since the late fifteenth century England had enjoyed 150 years of internal peace, but contemporaries were well aware of the effects of civil war on France in the last decades of the sixteenth century and on Germany since 1618. The English Civil Wars lasted for more than six years (with a break of twelve months) and, if the perspective is widened to Britain as a whole, bloodshed continued from the Bishops' Wars of 1639-40 to the final defeat of Charles II at Worcester in 1651. As a proportion of the total population, more men were involved and more died than during the Great War of 1914-18. In addition, the wars were fought on British soil with all the resulting destruction of property, dislocation of trade, and burden of incessant taxation. In short, civil war was nasty, brutish and destructive, and although contemporaries could not foresee the full horror of what lay ahead, many would have had more than an inkling about it.

It is important, therefore, to avoid any assumption that England slipped easily into war, or that such an outcome could be seriously contemplated when parliament met in 1640. The point is amply demonstrated by the optimistic assumptions of many of those who assembled at Westminster in the November of that year. What MPs expected was that the king's weakness would allow grievances to be redressed, bad advisers punished, and settlement to follow.

> Great expectance there is of a happy Parliament where the subject may have a total redress of all his grievances ...
> (From the *Diary* of Sir Henry Slingsby of Scriven, Yorkshire, November 1640 - Slingsby fought for the king in 1642.)
> 1 It is strange to note how we have slid into the beginnings of a civil war by one unexpected accident after another ... which have brought us thus far, as we scarce know how, but from paper combats ... we are now come to the question of raising forces.
> 5 (From a parliamentary speech by Bulstrode Whitelocke, summer 1642; Whitelocke served parliament throughout the war and the Interregnum)

Such comments, made by moderate men who were to find themselves on opposite sides in the coming conflict, illustrate key aspects of the situation that led to war in 1642. It is clear that in 1640 grievances against the king's recent policies were widespread; according to Slingsby, the Commons apply them to question all delinquents, all Projectors and Monopolisers, such as levied ship money, and such judges as gave it for law.

This is confirmed by Richard Baxter, a Puritan minister who was present in London and described the mood of the Commons:

1 They made many long and vehement speeches against the ship money, and against the judges that gave their judgement for it, and against the Et Cetera oath [in which ministers of the Church were required to accept the rules of the Laudian Church as containing
5 all that was necessary for salvation; both the ill-defined provisions and the extent of the claims raised difficulties for some] and the Bishops and Convocation that were the formers of it; but especially against the Lord Thomas Wentworth, Lord Deputy of Ireland, and Dr Laud, Archbishop of Canterbury, as evil counsellors who were
10 said to be the cause of all ...

It is apparent that Slingsby supported the widespread demand for redress, yet he was in fact to fight on the side of the king when the conflict came. Hence the list of grievances alone does not explain why men took up arms against their king, and it cannot be assumed that the crisis of 1640 would lead automatically to armed conflict. Nor do these sources suggest that war was either expected or intended. Thus the long-term problems and accumulation of grievances outlined in Chapter 1 and the evidence above explain the necessary precondition for the war, but not the advent of war itself. Not all of those who complained in 1640 were willing to take up arms against the king in 1642. Had they been prepared to do so, there could have been no civil war, for the king would have been unable to raise an army. It was precisely because some of those who disapproved of his actions up to 1640 were, in the end, prepared to defend him and his right to govern that a royalist 'side' emerged, and until this happened there was no question of military conflict. Even then, the existence of two 'sides' did not ensure that the crisis would come to a military conclusion, or even a conclusion at all at this particular time. A similar crisis in 1628-9 had been overcome by the king dissolving parliament and governing without reference to that body, but in 1640-1 parliament was not dissolved, and in 1642 the result was not government without parliament, but war.

There are, therefore, a number of questions to be addressed in considering how and why the crisis of 1640 ended in Civil War rather than settlement as expected by Slingsby and others like him. In the first place, there is a need to examine the demand for redress of grievances, the aims and intentions of those who led the campaign, and their failure to obtain the settlement they required. These issues are crucial to an understanding of both the process by which war became the most likely outcome of the crisis, and of the nature of the crisis itself. The initial aims of the participants reveal their attitudes and values, their concerns and priorities; and by tracing how these changed over the ensuing months it is possible to suggest some reasons why the outcome of their struggle was not as they intended. Secondly, we have to explain why the solidarity of their support declined, why, ultimately, two parties emerged, and what issues caused men of similar class, status and outlook to choose different sides. Finally it is necessary to explain why these parties felt compelled to resolve their differences quickly and decisively, by force if required, rather than to allow the situation to continue or to seek a long-term solution. Only by satisfactorily answering all these questions can we explain why men lost control of events, why war broke out against the wishes of so many, and why crisis became conflict.

The fact that the evidence available to historians is so often uncertain and inconclusive makes this a difficult task. Aims and intentions must be interpreted from actions that can be misunderstood, or that were deliberately devised to be misleading, and from statements that may or may not be acceptable at face value. Attitudes, values and the impact of events can be inferred from a range of sources, but the extent to which these may be applied to any individual inevitably varies. Herein, of course, lies one of the major causes of disagreements between historians.

2 Actions and Intentions, November 1640-May 1641

a) The King

Whatever Slingsby may have expected, there is little to suggest that redress of grievances was part of the king's agenda in November 1640. His ill-advised attempt to impose an adapted English Prayer Book on Scotland in 1637 had provoked his northern kingdom to rebellion, and he had found himself unable to raise and maintain effective forces from an English population which was almost equally discontented. As a result, he had been forced to conclude a treaty at Berwick in June 1639. The king's character and attitudes are clearly shown in the events that followed. Far from accepting the defeat of his religious policy (the Scottish Assemblies of 1638 and 1639 abolished both the Prayer Book and episcopacy in Scotland), Charles had set about obtaining the means to renew the war. Unable to raise enough revenue from existing sources and loans from loyal courtiers, he had summoned parliament in April 1640 (the Short Parliament), and when presented with lists of grievances to be redressed before supply was granted, had dissolved it in less than a month. Still oblivious to the necessity of compromise, he had raised new forces to meet a Scottish invasion, but these had been defeated at Newburn in August. With the Scots in possession of Newcastle and negotiations under way at Ripon, Charles had tried the expedient of a Great Council (of peers) at York, and only the Twelve Peers Petition for a new parliament had finally forced him to accept the necessity of summoning and dealing with that body. When the Treaty of Ripon had left the Scots in England and Charles bound to pay them £850 a day for their trouble, it had become clear that some concessions would have to be made. However, his demeanour in November revealed just how few and limited he intended those concessions to be.

When he opened the session of parliament on 3 November, Charles arrived at Westminster by river barge, thus avoiding the normal public procession and signalling his intention to complete the necessary business of obtaining parliamentary subsidies with as few concessions as possible. The opposition leaders had few illusions on the matter. John Pym's exhortation to the Scottish army around Newcastle to 'sit tight' revealed his awareness that only their presence in England, and the king's consequent need for money, had provided this opportunity to air the grievances that had accumulated since the bitter dissolution of 1629. Charles's experience of parliaments between 1625 and 1629, and their reluctance to accept responsibility for the necessary expenses of government, had given him little reason to view MPs as positive and reliable partners. The fact was that he had summoned this parliament out of necessity and as a last resort.

The significance of Charles's actions in this crisis was not that he behaved illegally or unconstitutionally, which he did not, but that he showed an inflexible perception of his own role as king and a dangerous absence of political skill. Charles did not doubt for one moment that it was his right to govern according to his conscience in both Church and state and in all three of his kingdoms. Control of the Church was an essential part of government, and quite apart from his own deep belief in the validity of the Anglican faith, there were difficulties in allowing Presbyterianism in Scotland while attacking Presbyterians in England. As Conrad Russell indicates in drawing attention to the problems of governing multiple kingdoms, it was not unreasonable in itself to seek to establish clear and uniform procedures throughout all three realms. In Charles's eyes, therefore, any opposition or resistance to his commands must be both unjustified and malicious. Armoured by his own convictions - not only his belief in the rightness of Laudian Anglicanism but also his sense of his own, God-given rights and duties as king - Charles was incapable of seeing and understanding the fears and concerns of others. Since he had no intention of restoring Catholicism, nor of governing without reference to law unless he was forced to do so by, for example, financial necessity, he could not comprehend the existence of fears about Catholic tyranny. Hence he was also incapable of genuine compromise. A fact that was perhaps even more serious in political terms was that he also lacked the confidence and flexibility to recognise when it would be advantageous to appear to compromise, if only temporarily. Because he believed his position to be right, Charles failed to recognise when circumstances required him to shift it. A clear example of this is his insistence that the Canons of 1640, which codified the church reforms made by Laud, be published and enforced despite the Scottish wars and the failure of the Short Parliament and against the advice of Laud himself. When finally forced to make concessions, for example in summoning this new parliament in November 1640, he did so with such obvious reluctance as to rob them of their worth and raise doubts about how far he could be trusted to keep whatever promises he made.

b) The Parliamentary Opposition

Unlike Slingsby, the opposition leadership was well aware of Charles's character and had considerable experience of both him and his methods. Three of them - John Pym, Sir Arthur Haselrig and Denzil Holles - had played a significant part in the parliamentary crisis of 1628-9 and had seen those who were responsible for the Three Resolutions of 1629 end in the Tower of London, where one, Sir John Eliot, had died after two years of imprisonment. For almost a decade they had been powerless to respond, but throughout the Scottish crisis of 1637-40 they had been in touch with the Scots, and it was this co-ordinated pressure that had led to the calling of parliament and the opportunity to present grievances. Now the same kind of pressure would be required to ensure that those grievances were adequately redressed, and to build in safeguards for the future. In particular, the feelings of the political nation within and outside parliament would have to be roused and maintained at a pitch where Charles would be forced by necessity, and even fear, to agree to measures that he would never willingly accept. According to Clarendon this strategy was clearly defined, at least in the mind of Pym, from the first meeting of the Long Parliament. He described a chance meeting with Pym in early November.

1 Mr Hyde [as Clarendon then was] met Mr Pym in Westminster
   Hall some days before the parliament, and conferring together
   upon the state of affairs, the other told him ... that they must now
   be of another temper than they were the last parliament [the Short
5 Parliament, 1640] ... that they had now an opportunity to make
   their country happy, by removing all grievances, and pulling up the
   causes of them by the roots, if all men would do their duties ... by
   which it was discerned that the warmest and boldest counsels
   would find a much better reception than those of a more temperate
10 nature; which fell out accordingly.

The campaign was well-organised. Speeches in the House of Commons were supported by a flood of petitions laying out complaints against unparliamentary taxation (especially Ship Money), the fines and exactions levied by the Star Chamber and other prerogative courts, changes in the Church, and the general 'countenancing of Popery' and 'discountenancing' of 'forward men in our religion', as Pym described the Puritan party. The focus of complaint was fixed upon the 'evil counsellors' who were to be held responsible, and whose fate would serve as a warning to others as well as depriving the king of his most effective servants. On 10 November the impeachment (trial by parliament) of Strafford was moved in the Commons and eight days later Archbishop Laud was also impeached. On 11 December the Root and Branch Petition for the reform of the Church was presented to the Commons, so that by the end of the year, within a month of parliament meeting, the main issues had been laid out and the first steps of remedial action could now be taken.

The first priority was the protection of parliament itself, and the Triennial Act, ensuring that parliaments would sit at least every three years, was presented to the king in February 1641. Complaining that 'you have taken the government almost to pieces and, I may say, it is almost off the hinges', Charles reluctantly gave his assent to the Act. By doing so he signalled that he could be pressured into making concessions, and when the opposition found in February and March that they lacked sufficient evidence and strength to impeach Strafford successfully, they sought to use the king's weakness once more. In April a Bill for Strafford's Attainder (a parliamentary declaration that he was guilty of treason, made without a formal trial) was introduced into the House of Commons, and both moral and physical persuasion was used to silence the doubters. As the crucial vote approached there were noisy scenes in London as the opposition and their allies organised a petition calling for Strafford's death; when the vote was taken in the Commons on 21 April only 59 MPs were prepared to vote against the Bill, although almost one third of the House had found it wise to be absent. Further intimidation ensued when the Bill moved to the House of Lords. Crowds gathered outside the House and those known to have opposed the Attainder were jostled and threatened - the result was that when a vote was taken, only 46 Lords were present, with only 11 voting against. Finally, when the king refused his assent, as he had promised Strafford he would, the mobs invaded Whitehall itself and the threat to the queen and his children was sufficient to destroy his resistance. On 9 May Charles signed away the life of his most effective minister, and in a telling comment written on the day of Strafford's execution, Laud described him as a prince who 'knew not how to be, or to be made, great'.

c) The King's Failure

These events emphasise the weakness of Charles's strategy in calling the Long Parliament. If he planned to gain financial support at the cost of a few concessions he had clearly misjudged the situation and, finding himself hemmed in, had no choice but to concede where necessary in order to buy time in which to find alternatives. These alternatives were not necessarily consistent. In April he flirted with the idea of a military solution when a group of army officers led by Sir John Ashburnham concocted a plot to release Strafford from the Tower, arrest the opposition leaders, and to disperse parliament. Within the same month Charles also considered buying off the opposition leadership by offering them power and positions in government. The suggestion came from the Duke of Bedford, Pym's patron and ally, that Charles should appoint the opposition leaders to office, Pym being named as Chancellor. Whether anything could have come of this plan is uncertain - it was forestalled by Bedford's untimely death in early May. What is clear is that Charles was desperately seeking a way out of his difficulties and, as so often, his willingness to consider contradictory methods robbed him of success in any one of them. As a reigning monarch carrying responsibility for government he had every right to consider a range of strategies, but his inconsistencies did help to build up a politically dangerous lack of trust. It is not clear how far he was involved in the army plot, but when it was revealed by Pym in early May it did the king enormous damage and greatly increased the distrust and suspicion with which he was regarded. The fact that Ashburnham kept his seat on the Privy Council far outweighed any denials that Charles had known or approved of the plan.

The intentions and errors of the king are relatively easy to discern, since this involves the study of the actions and beliefs of one man, whose character and weaknesses remained remarkably consistent throughout the period. The belief in his own Divine Right and the responsibilities which a king must therefore assume that motivated him in 1640-2 is the same belief that governed his behaviour in the 1620s and in the period leading up to his execution in 1649. The errors and vacillations of 1640-1 are also mirrored in those other crises. While different historians may emphasise different aspects of Charles's character and behaviour, and attribute different significance to these in comparison with other factors that influenced the outcome of events, there is broad agreement about what Charles wanted to achieve and why he failed to achieve it. Far more difficult to distinguish, and hence a matter of greater and more contentious debate, is the nature and intentions of the 'opposition' and its leaders.

d) The Nature of the Opposition

The modern concept of a parliamentary opposition, seeking to change government policy in a legitimate and acceptable way, was unknown in the seventeenth century. Government belonged to the king, and the ministers and officers who carried out its executive functions were his servants, appointed and dismissed by him according to his own choices and desires. The role of parliament was threefold - to inform the king of his subjects' needs and desires through the medium of petitioning, to pass such laws as were necessary for government to function, and to provide money through taxation for occasional and exceptional expenses. The concept of king-in-parliament, which underpinned the seventeenth-century constitution, related more to the rule of law than to any idea that parliament had a separate or restraining power on the king's choice of policy or ministers. The law made by the king through the institution of parliament was the highest law of the land, but it was still initiated, designed and devised by the king (or his chosen servants) and parliament's function in the process was legal and constitutional rather than political. The ancient constitution, to which Pym and his associates so eloquently and so often referred in their attempts to restrict Charles, was at most a system of common, or customary, law, supported by a number of specific documents such as Magna Carta, by which kings had agreed to grant and maintain certain rights and privileges, or 'liberties', in carrying out their function of governing. Powerful as was its appeal, the ancient constitution did not imply government by king and parliament as separate partners, and certainly had no place for a permanent, political opposition. Yet it is clear that in 1640 Charles was faced with a well-organised parliamentary group, determined to undo the work of his chosen ministers and force him to adopt both new men and new policies.

i) Explanations and Debates

The traditional explanation for this has been that the wealth and confidence of the House of Commons had greatly increased over the previous century and that the use made of parliament in the Reformation and the series of religious and political settlements that followed had given the institution a new status and its members a new political consciousness and experience. In the face, therefore, of a king who offended deeply held beliefs and prejudices, some members proved capable of utilising their financial power to assert their rights and force the king to operate within the limits of what was acceptable to the political nation. Other theories have suggested that the opposition was motivated by economic grievances, or by a resentment of a dominant and centralising Court. Whatever the motivation, these arguments all presented a picture of a numerous, united and coherent opposition party.

Recent research suggests that all such explanations involve a measure of over-simplification in seeking to explain an event as complex as the Civil War within a single theme. Coherent groups, whether inspired by principle or self-interest, are difficult to discern among MPs in 1640-2. According to Conrad Russell 'it has become painfully clear that it is impossible to interpret the Civil War as the clash of two clearly differentiated social groups or classes ... Nor are we trying to find causes for a conflict between a court and a country, or a government and an opposition'. Like most recent writers on the subject, he has refuted the traditional picture of a numerous opposition, united in a single purpose, and challenging an oppressive monarch for political power. Nevertheless, it is clear that Charles was dealing with something more than local or individual resentments, however numerous. Russell himself described an opposition leadership, which he labelled 'Pym's Junto', and it is inconceivable that such a group could have managed the parliamentary programme of 1640-1 without a large, if inconsistent, measure of support among MPs. John Adamson's work (see page 24) attributed much of their organisation to the influence of an aristocratic faction who were seeking power for themselves, but this does not explain the support that they received, nor what MPs thought they were achieving by their votes. While it has been generally agreed that explanations of the Civil War which are based on a single dominant issue are insufficient, the precise size, intentions and objectives of the 'opposition' remain a matter of some debate.

ii) The Significance of the Issue

The importance of this debate is that it implies quite different explanations, not only of why a war broke out, but also of what that war meant. If the opposition was widespread, reflecting deeply held beliefs and principles, then historians can speak plausibly of 'revolution' in English government, or at least of deep-seated and serious problems underlying the crisis. This does not mean that the opposition leaders were conscious revolutionaries - indeed most historians would accept the arguments of Russell and Ann Hughes that the opposition were mounting a defensive campaign against a king whom they thought was seeking to change traditional relationships in government. What was *potentially* revolutionary was their willingness to amend the constitution in order to resist him. If, however, the opposition amounted to little more than an aristocratic conspiracy, then the war must be seen as an act of rebellion arising from their failure to control the process that they had started. In either case, the war itself could be seen as accidental, or at least unintended. What is at issue is whether the aims of the opposition were to reform, or merely to take control of, the existing system of government.

    At first sight, then, we are faced with conflicting and incompatible interpretations which have a considerable bearing on the central issue of why war broke out in 1642, and on the events that followed in the next two decades. As we know, historical events are rarely to be explained by any single factor, deriving instead from the interaction of a number of issues, and while there continues to be room and cause for debate, the different interpretations can, on closer examination, be largely reconciled. It may well be the case, for example, that a group of opposition peers sought to use the anger of the Commons to attain power for themselves, and that influential MPs were content to accept their leadership. Indeed, given the structure of seventeenth-century society, it would be surprising if this did not occur. This does not mean that the causes of that anger were not genuine and significant, nor that the leaders, aristocratic or otherwise, did not share the beliefs and concerns that lay behind it.

Nor is it necessary to find a single, all-embracing issue in order to explain the apparent unity achieved by those seeking to rally and direct the resentment which existed. A man whose main concern was religion might have no difficulty in sympathising with those who disliked the encroachments of central power over local government, if that power was seen as the source of both the political and religious policies which were disliked. The opponents of Laud and the enemies of Strafford had much in common, and might well be expected to make common cause in the right conditions. According to Richard Baxter, who observed the MPs at the time, it was precisely a mixture of grievances of this kind that created widespread discontent in 1640 and in that sense it was Charles himself who laid the basis of opposition support. His financial policies, religious reforms, use of the prerogative courts, and extension of central power in all his three kingdoms gave rise to a range of grievances that affected most men in one way or another and created the potential for resistance. What made his position so dangerous was the existence of leaders whose political skills and influence enabled them to hold the shifting mass together, and whose own political or religious objectives may have gone beyond those that they publicly expressed.

iii) Assessment - The Nature and Origins of the Opposition

It is, therefore, possible to resolve a number of apparent conflicts of interpretation and draw some broad conclusions concerning the nature of the 'opposition' and their part in the outbreak of war. It can be said, for example, that there existed within the House of Commons in 1640 a coherent opposition group - Conrad Russell's 'Pym's junto' - which was organised, employed clearly defined tactics, and had specific aims. There is room for debate about how extensively the group was organised and about the role of the lords with whom it was closely associated, but there is no doubt that its origins as a group can be traced back to the political crises of the 1620s. By 1640 its centre was John Pym, a skilful political tactician who had first entered parliament in 1620. He had participated in the Commons' Protestation (against James's refusal to allow them to debate foreign policy) of 1621, being placed under house arrest for five days as a result, and in the attack on the king's favourite, the Duke of Buckingham. Resentment of the duke's power and anger at his incompetence in the direction of foreign policy had brought together a group of lords and MPs - the Earl of Warwick, Lord Saye and Sele, and Sir John Eliot among them - who continued to oppose Charles's high-handedness after the favourite had been assassinated. They organised the Petition of Right in 1628 and a year later we find these names joined with others - Holles, Valentine, Hampden and Pym - in the crisis that produced the Three Resolutions of 1629. The crises of the 1620s, therefore, established personal friendships and contacts among these men and also provided a measure of political and parliamentary experience which was used to good effect in 1640.

What they had in common was a belief that the law of the land was binding on the king as well as his subjects and a religious outlook that was Puritan, or at least strongly anti-Catholic. In both areas, Charles's policies offended and frightened them and his actions in 1629, and after, increased their fears. The dissolution of parliament and the king's obvious reluctance to call another, the attempt to gain financial independence in the 1630s, and, above all, Arminianism in the Church and Catholic influence at Court, convinced those who were already suspicious of Charles that he sought to establish a continental-style and possibly Catholic, absolutism. It is difficult to trace their activities in the eleven year absence of parliament between 1629 and 1640, but there is evidence of continuing contact of some kind. Pym and Bedford were both directors of the Providence Island Company, while Hampden's initiation of the Ship Money test case in 1637 was certainly not the act of a man working alone. These links are not sufficient to constitute a political organisation, but they did make it easier for plans and strategies to be evolved when the need and opportunity arose. There is little doubt that after the outbreak of rebellion in Scotland in 1638, contacts were established between the Scottish Covenanters and Pym's associates in England, notably through Nathaniel Fiennes, son and heir of Lord Saye and Sele (a title that often confuses as it seems to refer to more than one man - but it is a single title).

The experience of the Short Parliament in 1640 finalised the formation of a group, led in the Commons by Pym, who played an active role in preventing the granting of supplies. It was probably at this time that they began to develop both their organisation and their strategy. When Charles ordered the arrest of Lords Warwick, Brooke, and Saye and Sele (along with leading members of the Commons) after the dissolution of the Short Parliament, he was indicating those whom he believed to be the leaders of a faction, which is how he would have regarded them. The weeks that followed the opening of the Long Parliament revealed the extent and effectiveness of this opposition group. The main forum was the House of Commons, although contact and consultation with the opposition lords was clearly maintained. Pym's proposal of a Committee to consider the nation's grievances provided a powerful weapon against pressure and manipulation by the

Court and care was taken to secure control of this and other important committees.

Opposition strategy was gradually revealed in the series of impeachments and bills proposed by different members of the group in the winter of 1640-1. Proceedings in parliament were supported by outside pressure and contacts - the petitions and demonstrations in London that accompanied major debates and votes such as those involved in the attainder of Strafford were undoubtedly organised and orchestrated to achieve maximum effect. Contacts with the Scots had already reached the point of treason. It is clear, therefore, that Charles had to deal with an organised opposition that was skilled in political tactics. Although this organised core was small in numbers, it was able to direct and manipulate the anger of the parliament and nation for its own political purposes. What remains a matter of debate is the nature and extent of those purposes - what, in fact, the opposition was trying to achieve.

iv) Assessment - The Aims and Intentions of the Opposition

The leaders claimed to be trying merely to restore the balance of the constitution and the Protestant Church in order to protect the political and religious 'liberties' that had been undermined by the activities of 'evil counsellors' who had come between the king and his people. However, it is impossible to accept these stated purposes entirely at face value. The attack on Strafford and Laud, for example, portrayed the two men as the source of a conspiracy whose purpose was the destruction of English 'liberties', and treated the king as their innocent dupe. But it is inconceivable, given their previous experience of him, that they did not see Charles I as the real author of their difficulties. It was just that the conventions of the time and the need to carry the support of the less sophisticated backbenchers made it impossible to attack the king directly. By concentrating attention on an unpopular minister like Strafford, Pym was able to rally the support of future royalists like Digby and Slingsby for a tactic which, in practice, undermined the king's free choice of advisers. The fact was that the opposition did not trust Charles and was seeking to bind him for the future. Given the number of lawyers in the opposition ranks, they were surely aware of the extent to which legislation such as the Triennial Act was adding to the powers of parliament and reducing those of the king, thereby changing, rather than restoring, the constitutional balance. Thus, interpreting their actions in the light of political attitudes and pressures of the time, it becomes necessary at the very least to redefine the opposition's aims as a desire to restore the balance of the constitution and the Protestant Church by depriving the king of the means to destroy it - his chosen advisers and the free exercise of his powers.

In practical terms, this meant new restrictions on the king's prerogative and an extension of the powers of parliament. And while there is no evidence to suggest that they were trying to achieve this for its own sake, it was a necessity which a man like Pym could happily accept. Nevertheless, he was on dangerous ground. Although widespread resentment of Charles's policies had built up during the absence of parliament, most MPs sought no more than the redress of grievances through the traditional channels, such as parliamentary petitions. They were realistic enough to know that Charles might have to be pressured into granting concessions, but changes in the constitution or in the king's governing functions were looked upon as dangerous innovations. In political terms, Pym's priority had to be to present the necessity of change in such a way as to carry the more naive, or the more conservative, backbenchers with him.

However, one question which remains is the extent to which personal ambition influenced and motivated the opposition leadership in their plans. Clarendon and other royalists had no doubt that this was a major factor, and the fact that Pym, Bedford and St John had worked out a plan to reorganise royal finances suggests that the king's proposal in May 1641 that they accept government office, was neither unexpected nor unwelcome. What is crucial in assessing the nature of the opposition is to decide whether this ambition constituted their primary motive, and the available evidence suggests that it was not. Bedford was a man born to political life by virtue of his title and position and Pym was an astute and experienced politician, but both appear to have held strong and sincere religious beliefs, to the point of considering emigration in 1637-8 rather than accept the reforms instituted by Laud. In that context a willingness to accept office in the only form of government that they knew is as indicative of a desire to serve their cause as it is evidence of any greed for personal power. Government lay with the king, and only by gaining positions in the king's service could they establish a government that they, and others, could trust. Whether or not they could have succeeded in restraining or influencing Charles is quite another matter, but in the spring of 1641 both Bedford and Pym may reasonably have believed that this represented the only possible route to the settlement they desired.

It can therefore be suggested that the 'opposition' to Charles and his government consisted of a small, organised and coherent group of parliamentarians (both in the Lords and the Commons) who were able to orchestrate and channel the widespread desire for redress of grievances in both Church and State towards the constitutional change which they deemed necessary. They were capable of planning and carrying out a parliamentary programme and they intended to use their political and financial powers to force the king to adopt new policies and advisers, and to establish the future security of their parliament, their religion, their 'Liberties' and themselves. In pursuit of these goals they were willing to use propaganda, persuasion, manipulation and intimidation. Until the execution of Strafford in May 1641 their story is one of remarkable success.

3 The First Turning-point: The Death of Strafford

The execution of Strafford marks a crucial stage in the shift from crisis to conflict. It appeared that if the king could be induced by pressure to break his word publicly and sacrifice the life of his most effective minister and a loyal servant, then there was little that could not be gained if the right kind of pressure could be maintained. Thus the opposition leaders were confirmed in their strategy and the pattern of changes to be forced upon a reluctant monarch was set for the spring and summer of 1641. In May an 'Act against the Dissolution of this Parliament without its own Consent' was passed, in July the king accepted the abolition of the prerogative courts of Star Chamber and High Commission, and in August Ship Money was declared illegal. In each of these cases Charles accepted a significant reduction of his own power and independence.

At the same time, however, the game had become more dangerous. In order to remove Strafford the opposition had been forced to use the device of attainder and to threaten and humiliate the king. A more forgiving monarch than Charles would have felt justified in punishing those responsible when he had the opportunity, and it is not surprising that he considered the use of force to solve his problems. The army plot revealed in May provided clear evidence of his willingness to do so. It was reinforced by the queen's advice to call on her brother, the King of France, for money and arms. By the end of May 1641 there can have been little doubt in the minds of Pym and his associates that if their pressure should falter and their campaign to restrict the king's powers fail, they would pay with their fortunes and probably with their lives. According to Conrad Russell, 'an acceptable settlement, meaning one which would have left both Charles and Pym's junto confident that they would be alive and at liberty in twelve months' time, had become remote by March 1641, and became a total impossibility between 3 and 12 May 1641'. This did not mean that Civil War became inevitable at that date - a solution of some kind could still have been forced upon one party by the other - but it is unlikely that a settlement to which both would willingly agree could have been reached.

If this is the case, it is perhaps necessary to ask why the opposition adopted such a high risk strategy. Russell's explanation is that their Scottish allies required Strafford's death as a condition of continuing support. Whether or not this was the case - the evidence is not conclusive - the junto had plenty of reason to fear Strafford's determination and effectiveness as a minister, and it is probably the case that, had Charles listened to his advice more often in the years before 1640, their present opportunity to reverse or restrict his policies would not have existed. The future royalist, Lord Digby, declared him to be 'the most dangerous minister, the most insupportable to free subjects, that can be charactered'. The likelihood is that genuine fear of Strafford's abilities as well as the underlying strategy of attacking the king through his servants would have made his death a necessity, with or without Scottish pressure.

Strafford's execution and the means of attaining it, therefore, made a genuine settlement of differences impossible. The opposition had gone too far ever to retract, and both they and the king knew it. Even if Charles should agree to a compromise, the opposition leadership would not dare to trust his word. Hence the only acceptable settlement for Pym and his associates would either be one in which the king's power was so limited as to render him unable to punish them, or one in which parliament's powers were sufficient to protect them. For their own safety, and because they could not, and did not, trust the king to uphold concessions that had been forced from him, they could not afford to be content with the political and constitutional gains which had been made by the early summer of 1641. They had already succeeded in removing the abuses of the past, and their apparent authors, but to rest secure they had also to ensure that they could not reappear. Since the real, but politically untouchable, author of the problem was the king himself, only by binding and limiting his powers could they ensure future security. By executing Strafford and impeaching Laud the opposition had deprived the king, and themselves, of convenient scapegoats. They were therefore forced openly to attack the powers of the king, in a way that some of their own supporters might well find unacceptable.

4 The Loss of Parliamentary Unity, May 1641-January 1642

a) Unity and its Problems

The opposition leaders' difficulties lay in the interaction of three factors. In the first place, they were now undeniably engaged in a power struggle with the king which they could not afford to lose. Secondly, any progress in this struggle would involve limiting the king's powers and hence encroaching on his valid and accepted prerogatives. Thirdly, and here lay the core of their problem, they could only succeed in doing this by maintaining the unity of parliament, or at least of the Commons. This meant that they were dependent on the support of a number of men, like Slingsby, who did not fully share nor even understand the objectives that they were pursuing. Through experience and interest, the opposition leaders had acquired a skill and even a political professionalism which set them apart from the majority of MPs, who were for the most part country gentlemen and merchants chosen to represent the needs and interests of their town or locality in the traditionally limited and occasional functions of parliament. Nowhere in their experience, nor in their concept of government by king-in-parliament, was there an independent role for parliament. Yet this was what the campaign to restrict and limit Charles in the free exercise of his powers was inexorably creating. The further the opposition travelled in this direction, the more likely they were to shed much-needed supporters along the way.

The opposition campaign was mostly conducted with as much caution as the circumstances allowed, increasing only gradually the power of parliament to restrict and constrain the king. The impeachment of ministers such as Laud and Strafford was not new, and the Triennial Act of February 1641 gave parliament the right to sit each third year but did not preclude the king from calling and dissolving it as he wished within that framework. Moreover, it did nothing to change its powers when it did sit. The execution of Strafford might make it more difficult for the king to find ministers to carry out his plans, but it only showed parliament's ability to call bad ministers to account in a similar way to the old device of impeachment.

In June 1641 a more significant step was taken with the presentation to the king of the Ten Propositions, which attempted to define rules and procedures for the future conduct of government, including a right of parliament to approve (or, by implication, reject) the king's choice of ministers and councillors. Important as this claim was, it was still couched in suitably respectful terms. It was requested that the king should 'take into his Council for managing of the great affairs of this kingdom such officers and counsellors as his people and parliament may have just cause to confide in'. For the politically naive, who might take such a request at face value, there was little that could be considered offensive in this. Only a consideration of how the arrangement might work in practice and of what might be the case if parliament did not 'confide in' a chosen minister would bring out the vital implications of the king's agreement to such a proposition.

Through such careful drafting and presentation of their plans the opposition were able, for the most part, to carry the majority of MPs with them. But the further they progressed, the more difficult the task became. By the summer of 1641 there were ominous cracks appearing in the facade of unity. Some, like Gervase Holles and Lord George Digby, were disturbed by the means used to pursue Strafford, while others, like Edward Hyde, feared that the balance of power in government was being too greatly disturbed. Many of the back-benchers felt that their purposes had been achieved, and saw no reason to linger unnecessarily in the heat and squalor of London in summer when their own affairs required their attention. It is important not to exaggerate divisions at this stage, but there are signs that by the early summer of 1641 the opposition campaign was beginning to falter. This was just as they began to address that most contentious and divisive of all the issues facing them, the control and organisation of the Church.

b) Religious Issues and Divisions

'We all agree' stated Lord George Digby in a speech concerning the Root and Branch Petition in December 1640, '... that a Reformation of Church government is most necessary'. There is no doubt that religious grievances played a large part in bringing about the crisis of 1640, but it is equally clear that the nature and extent of these grievances varied. The Anglican Church rested on a compromise, and like all compromises it met with criticism from a variety of quarters. Since the reign of Elizabeth there had been those who considered that the Reformation had stopped short and who wished to carry on the task of purifying the Church of popish remnants and practices. They compared the discipline and liturgy (services and prayers) of England unfavourably with those practised in the Presbyterian system of Scotland. With the accession in England of James I in 1603 the comparisons became more acute, but with considerable skill the new king forged a compromise to suit his political needs and by cautious steps began to bring the Scottish system into line with the English use of bishops as the means of maintaining royal control. The essential core of this compromise lay in the undoubted and unchallengeable acceptance by the king, and the vast majority of his bishops, of Calvinist doctrines. These were the Protestant beliefs laid down and practised by John Calvin in the Church that he had founded in Geneva. At their heart was the idea of predestination, a belief that salvation could not be earned or chosen by individuals (as Catholics and Arminians taught) but was a free gift from God, granted to those whom he had been chosen and pre-destined to be saved and to live eternally among his 'saints'. Whatever their concerns about rituals, ceremonies and the absence of Presbyterian discipline, the critics of the Church had no need to doubt its Protestant identity and its total rejection of Rome and all its works. It was the destruction of this compromise by Charles and Archbishop Laud that gave rise to religious grievances in England, as well as provoking open rebellion in Scotland.

The discontent created can be categorised at three broad levels. At the highest level were the small minority of people who favoured a fully Calvinist system, with the Church purified and a discipline administered by ministers and lay elders as in Scotland. A much larger number of people (and MPs) desired a simplified form of worship and an emphasis on a preaching and teaching ministry, but had no objection to the use of bishops as a form of administration. Beyond this, the vast majority of the English feared and detested the name and idea of popery as a threat to their liberties, their souls, and their national survival.

The achievement of Charles and Laud had been to offend at all of these levels. Their interpretation of Arminian doctrines involved creating an authoritarian Church, welcoming all without making a distinction between 'saints' and sinners, promising salvation through the Church rather than through prayer and Bible-reading, and utilising set prayers and ceremonies to create a sense of reverence described by Laud as 'the beauty of holiness'. While this was attractive to some, it did represent, in both doctrine and organisation, a step closer to the ideas of the Catholic Church. Thus it threatened the established practices and doctrines of the Church and seemed, deliberately or otherwise, to open the way for the triumph of the imagined Catholic conspiracy which (in the eyes of contemporaries) threatened not only their religion but their political liberties as well. Hence the broad agreement to which Digby referred. The nation knew what it did not like. And it did not like Laud and his works. Nor were the majority of MPs prepared to accept the political role that the bishops had played. Laud's role as a Privy Councillor and the appointment of Bishop Juxon as Lord Treasurer from 1636 were greatly resented, as was the existence of a solid block of automatic royalist support in the House of Lords through the presence of the 26 bishops there. So strong was this resentment of episcopal interference in secular politics that in January 1641 Charles had agreed to dismiss them from government office, thus accepting a significant restriction on his freedom of choice. But he had insisted on retaining them in the Upper House. By 1 May, even before the execution of Strafford, the Commons had passed a bill to exclude them from the House of Lords, which was finally rejected by the Upper House in June. Nevertheless the matter was pursued and in February 1642, when the Upper House was more under the control of the king's opponents, the Clerical Disabilities Act finally removed the bishops' temporal authority (in matters outside the Church) and seats in the Lords.

To this extent - but only to this extent - religious grievances united the nation in opposition to the king and his archbishop. To agree what they did not want was a simple matter: to agree on what should replace it was far more difficult. The alternative proposed in the Root and Branch Bill which was introduced in the Commons at the end of May 1641 was a Presbyterian system similar to that which had been restored in Scotland. But, while many MPs and their constituents espoused Calvinist doctrines and practices, they had no intention of handing over the discipline of the Church and the right of judgement over their morals and behaviour to churchmen of any kind. Indeed, part of their dislike of Laud stemmed from resentment at clerical pretensions, as illustrated by his attack on lay control of lectureships and many benefices. As Digby put it, to accept Presbyterian discipline would mean that 'instead of every Bishop we put down in a Diocese, we shall set up a Pope in every Parish'. Other, perhaps more central, concerns can be seen in an extract from the diary of Sir Henry Slingsby.

1 I went with the Bill for their taking of [the bishops'] votes in the

House of Peers and for meddling with temporal affairs but I was against the Bill for taking away the function and calling of Bishops ... I could never be of that opinion that the government of the
5 Church, as it is now established by Bishops and Archbishops to be of absolute necessity, so that the taking of them away should quite overturn the state and essence of the christian church; but I am of the opinion that the taking of them out of the Church ... may be of dangerous consequence to the peace of the Church ... considering
10 that this government hath continued from the Apostles ... it were not safe to make alteration from so ancient a beginning.

For Slingsby the existence of episcopacy was not a matter of faith but of political and social discipline. The Church was an institution of state and a major form of social control in a society that lacked effective methods of law enforcement. The obedience of the people depended on acceptance of the social hierarchy and the teaching of deference - if that was destroyed in the Church, where would it be threatened next? It is significant that, when war came, both Digby and Slingsby would fight on the side of the king. Edward Hyde, who became the leader of a moderate royalist group in the Commons also cited the introduction of the Root and Branch Bill as crucial in his decision to break with the opposition party. Not for the last time, the adherents of Presbyterian discipline were to find their schemes rejected by a large number of their countrymen, many of whom shared their religious preferences in other ways. While some were merely reacting against clerical control of their lives and behaviour, others, like Slingsby, had far wider concerns regarding the role and place of the Church. While Slingsby disliked the bishops' claim to a power received directly from God, he found Laud's emphasis on ritual and ceremony preferable to the Puritan insistence on preaching, teaching and the importance of individual conscience, which he regarded as politically dangerous. While others, including Hyde, did not go this far, there was among the governing class which made up the parliament, a widespread conservatism which regarded the Anglican Church, headed by the king and governed by bishops, as a guarantee of stability in society.

This reaction was considerably sharpened in 1641 by the emergence, in London at least, of a radical underworld which confirmed their worst fears. The weakening of episcopal control that had resulted from the attack on the bishops' powers had permitted the small groups of puritan separatists, who had previously met in secret, to operate far more openly. In addition, the breakdown of censorship had released a flood of pamphlets expressing radical ideas about religion and society. Nothing could illustrate more clearly to a conservative mind the dreadful consequences of removing the power and control of the Church over the people and of the bishops over the Church.

Religious problems as seen from both sides of the political and religious spectrum

In that sense the rejection in June of Root and Branch reform, entailing the abolition of episcopacy, was part of a wider conservative reaction which was beginning to take shape. To the extent that it gathered and focussed conservative unease about how far the opposition leaders were prepared to go in their struggle with the king, the religious issue was a major factor in the emergence, in the middle of 1641, of a king's party which could significantly alter the likely outcome of the crisis.

c) The Emergence of the Royalists

In November 1640 civil war was impossible because the king did not have a party large enough to fight for him. By the summer of 1641 this was changing, and by January 1642 when Charles attempted to arrest the Five Members he clearly believed that he was strong enough to risk an open breach. Therefore, if we are to explain why war eventually broke out, we need to understand why, by 1642, many were ready to support him and why the king was sufficiently aware of this to bring matters to a head. It is not merely a matter of explaining why, once war was imminent, many were drawn back to old loyalties or found themselves unable to commit the sin of rebellion. If we are to understand why war became possible at all, we need to explain the emergence, by the autumn of 1641, of a sizeable group of people who were prepared to resist Pym's junto in parliament and to try to rally support for the king.

It is also important to emphasise that the men in question were not attempting to undo the achievements of 1640 and early 1641. Led by Edward Hyde and Lucius Carey, Lord Falkland, they sought a compromise which would restrain the king from further unconstitutional acts, guarantee the rule of law and the rights of parliament, and leave intact the valid powers of the king in both Church and State. Their concept of government was the harmonious partnership of king-in-parliament. Hence one reason for their emergence was the growing perception that by June 1641, with steps such as the Ten Propositions, the opposition was going too far in destroying the balance that they sought. In this sense the moderate royalists were true conservatives, seeking to preserve what they saw as the traditional balance between government, law, and individual or local rights and liberties. Thus they were further offended and confirmed in their dislike of Pym's junto by the Militia Bill and the Grand Remonstrance of late 1641 (see page 53).

Conservatism was also a major influence on their religious outlook. Yet for many royalists there was more involved than a preference for traditional forms and a concern to maintain spiritual and intellectual control over the masses. Without accepting the high-flown claims of Laud that bishops inherited their authority in a direct line from the Apostles and thus from Christ himself, there were many who had come to value the Anglican faith for its own sake. The balanced rationalism of the Elizabethan settlement had been successfully defended by Richard

Hooker just before his death in 1600. In his *Laws of Ecclesiastical Polity* he had argued that Anglican practice truly reflected the spirit of early Christianity, shorn of the corrupting influence of popery, and that the functions of the bishops and the remaining ceremonies were to ensure good order and decency in worship. As such, they were therefore neither necessary for salvation, nor any barrier to it, and men could maintain their own opinions while accepting the need for the monarch to make decisions regarding their use in a national church.

These arguments struck a chord among men who were coming to the conclusion that religious differences should be minimised. The intellectual development of the early seventeenth century represented by Sir Francis Bacon and the growing interest in the scientific study of the natural world was helping to create a distaste for both superstition and religious bigotry. It was no coincidence that both Hyde and Falkland had been members of an intellectual circle which met to discuss such issues at Great Tew in Wiltshire. There were men on both sides of the political divide of 1642 who shared this outlook, and in this sense Hyde and Falkland had much in common with Lord Brooke, who raised a regiment for parliament in 1642, and the Puritan intellectual, John Milton. In their case, a rational approach to religion led eventually to a belief in religious toleration. For Hyde and others it was allied to a preference for the middle way adopted by the Elizabethan and Jacobean Church. While they rejected the clericalism of Laud, they had no intention of replacing it with the Presbyterian clericalism of the Root and Branch Bill. This emotion was most clearly expressed by Digby (see pages 44-45) but it was also a factor in the affection and loyalty felt by other royalists for the moderate, balanced, Anglican compromise that had been familiar to them before Laud. The survival of Anglican practice and use of the Prayer Book throughout the war and Interregnum, is evidence of its popularity and enduring support at all levels of society.

Thus conservatism, based on a desire for what was believed to be the traditional balance in Church and State, seems to have been of crucial importance in the formation of a royalist group in parliament. However, Conrad Russell has pointed to another dimension which combined and overlapped with these views - a resistance to Scottish interference and dictation. In Russell's view the Scots had 'an imperial vision' in which English practice in Church and State would be adapted to that of Scotland, and in which the imposition of Presbyterian practice in the Church was a key element. There is certainly no doubt that the Scottish Covenanters - the Puritans or Presbyterians who had led the rebellion of 1637 and the subsequent invasion of England - did desire to spread Presbyterian practice to England. They made it the price of their support for the opposition in 1640-1, the condition of their alliance with parliament in 1643, and in their agreement with the king in December 1647. According to Russell, 'Those who emerged as anti-Scots in the first four months of the Long Parliament were Sir John Holland, Sir William Widdrington, Sir William Pennyman, Sir John Strangeways, Charles Price, Dr.Turner, John Selden, Edward Hyde, Sir Ralph Hopton, Arthur Capel and George Digby. Save for Selden and Sir John Holland, this list is almost a roll-call of the inner ring of the royalist party in the Commons and it merely confirms the point that the list of anti-Scots soon clearly included Falkland, Culpepper, Kirton and Waller. The Royalist party was an anti-Scottish party before it was a Royalist party'.

There were, therefore, a number of different but probably overlapping reasons for the growth of a royalist group during the summer and autumn of 1641. Most significantly there was a dislike of the lengths to which Pym and his allies were taking the campaign and of the methods they were employing. There was fear for the balance of the constitution and of popular involvement in political activity. In addition, there was affection for the Anglican Church stripped of Laudian pretensions and dislike of clericalism of all kinds and particularly in its Scottish version. It is clear that the leaders of the group shared many of these perceptions, although which of them weighed most heavily with the uncommitted is more difficult to say. There is little doubt that, given real control over the king's actions, advisers such as Hyde and Sir Edward Nicholas (who became Secretary of State in 1641) could have won over large numbers and could probably have isolated the opposition. Their failure was largely caused by the king's tendency, at crucial times, to listen to less balanced advice. Thus from June 1641 to January 1642 the uncommitted majority probably remained uncommitted, suspicious of opposition schemes for the Church and later the militia, offended by the king's resort to more violent solutions in the Second Army Plot of June 1641 (revealed in October) and in the attempted arrest of the Five Members in January 1642 (an act to which Hyde was bitterly opposed).

d) The Junto and its Difficulties

Members of the opposition were, therefore, able to maintain a considerable measure of support and sympathy, but faced an increasingly desperate struggle to preserve the parliamentary unity that they required if they were to guarantee the safety of their reforms and of themselves. In these circumstances, it is necessary to ask why the opposition leadership persisted with reforms and measures in two areas where their support was clearly weak - the abolition of bishops in favour of a Presbyterian system, and the further restriction of the king's power. The latter can be explained fairly simply, for it was impossible to stop the process that had been begun until there was some guarantee of the permanence of what had been achieved. Unless and until they could trust Charles, or limit his powers so tightly that he could not undo their work (or threaten their lives and estates), the members of the opposition were bound to continue with what they had started. The religious issue was more complex, involving a number of possible motives, some based on deeply held convictions, others upon personal or political necessity. In the first place, for many of the opposition leaders religious reform was not a matter of politics but of principle. For men such as Oliver St. John and Nathaniel Fiennes the abolition of episcopacy was an issue of conscience. Some of them believed in the necessity of Presbyterian discipline, but for others the strongest argument was the corrupting influence of bishops who obstructed preaching and encouraged idolatry. For those who believed that the way to God was through private prayer, the study of the Bible, and the teaching of God's word, the rituals and organisation imposed by the bishops were a positive barrier to individual salvation and conspired to maintain ignorance and darkness in society. They believed that only when this barrier was removed would true religion flourish and the 'reformation of manners' in society begin. By no means did all of the opposition share this view. Some political tacticians favoured Root and Branch reform because it would serve to weaken the king's control of the Church. There was also another, more compelling reason for presenting the scheme to parliament - as indicated above, it was the price demanded by the Scottish Covenanters for their continued support, and without them the opposition would be lost. It should not be forgotten that the continued existence of the Long Parliament derived from the king's need for money to maintain his agreement with the Scots. If their support should be withdrawn, then the hopes of the opposition, and probably their lives and fortunes would be lost with it.

Thus, for a variety of reasons and motives, the opposition was committed to the abolition of episcopacy and would be unable to give way on this matter even if it cost them the chance of a settlement or vital parliamentary support. It is impossible to be sure which of these concerns weighed most heavily. John Morrill has emphasised the importance of religion as a motive within the parliamentarian group, and has argued that it is underestimated in Russell's attribution of such great influence to the Scots. There is no doubt that, again and again in the events of the Civil War period, religious zeal distinguished those who were willing to push on to adopt ever more extreme or dangerous measures from those who sought to compromise or to put a brake on the process of change. What Morrill calls 'Puritan dynamism' was a real and important element in parliamentarian thinking. In terms of the Root and Branch Bill and the influence of the Scots, it is impossible to be sure, except in individual cases, which motive was paramount. It should also be pointed out that the Scottish Covenanters were themselves motivated by Puritan convictions and a missionary zeal to spread the true faith. Whatever the precise mixture of motives behind its presentation, the rejection of the Root and Branch Bill by the House of Commons in June

1641 was a severe blow to Pym and his associates, and marked the opening of a religious division which, more clearly than any other single issue, defined the opposing parties or 'sides' into which the nation would fall within a year. By the summer of 1641, therefore, there were signs of a weakening in the opposition leaders' position and an improvement in that of the king. Encouraged by this to see a possible way out of his difficulties, Charles announced in August that he would visit Scotland in order to ratify the Treaty of Ripon. What his real intentions were is unclear, but there were signs of the emergence of a royalist party in Edinburgh and his choice of the royalist Earl of Morton as his Chancellor in August 1641 suggests that he may have been trying to build up their strength. If so, he acted with a lack of political tact, promising co-operation with the Scottish parliament on the one hand and selecting officers who were offensive to them on the other. The result was that he failed to establish the support that he required but demonstrated once more to the opposition and the uncommitted in both kingdoms that he could not be trusted to keep his word. For the opposition leaders in London this was a time of great difficulty and danger. Their fears of Charles's activities in Scotland were widely shared among their sympathisers. According to Lucy Hutchinson, the wife of the staunchly Puritan Colonel John Hutchinson,

1 The king's design in going to Scotland was variously conjectured; but this was a certain effect of it, that it retarded all the affairs of the government of England, which the king had put into such disorder that it was not an easy task to reform what was amiss and redress
5 the real grievances of the people.

In September came the parliamentary recess, a time when the opposition leaders were at their most vulnerable to attack or arrest, and it was not unreasonable that they feared for their lives and liberties if the king should succeed in freeing himself of his problems with the Scots. If he could freely use the military strength at his disposal then they might well find themselves seized as rebels and traitors, the parliament dismissed, and the reforms that they had achieved thus far reversed and destroyed. That this did not occur can be attributed to two factors. The first was Charles's lack of judgement and political skill in dealing with the Scots. The second arose from his kingdom across the water - the outbreak of rebellion in Ireland at the end of October 1641.

5 The Second Turning-point: The Irish Rebellion

In the early autumn of 1641 an Irish population which had seen much of its land pass into the hands of English and Scottish settlers and had suffered the heavy hand of Lord Deputy Strafford, seized the opportunity offered by his demise and the king's preoccupation with other matters, and rose in armed revolt. It is difficult to exaggerate either the impact or the significance of the Irish rebellion in the sequence of events which led from the crisis of 1640-1 to the war of 1642. For the English Protestant, the Irish combined the menace of an uncivilised race with the demonology of popery. As the stories of Catholic atrocities against their Protestant neighbours filtered across the water through October and November, the fear and tension rose and with it the need for action to suppress the rebels. Yet, to the fury of MPs, the king chose to linger in Scotland, not returning south to an England rife with rumours of Irish invasion until 17 November. In Yorkshire church services were interrupted with the news that the Irish had landed in Lancashire, had already reached Rochdale and would shortly be in Bradford. To some extent this reflects the deep-seated and irrational fear of popery that existed in seventeenth-century England, but fear of Catholic invasion did have some foundation in reality. It was not that the Irish rebels themselves constituted a threat to England and its government, but that Ireland as a base for attack by Catholic powers such as France and Spain was a real possibility, particularly if they should be invited by a king who was under threat from his parliament and a king with a French Catholic wife.

In these circumstances Charles lost both credibility and his chances of ridding himself of a troublesome parliament. According to Richard Baxter,

1 there was nothing that with the people wrought so much [had so much effect] as the Irish massacre and rebellion ... This filled all England with a fear both of the Irish and of the Papists at home ... And when they saw the English Papists join with the king against
5 the parliament it was the greatest thing that ever alienated them from the king.

An army had to be raised to suppress the rebels and an army must be paid for - and only parliamentary subsidies could provide the necessary finance. Accordingly Charles asked the Commons for help in raising forces and thereby presented the opposition with an impossible dilemma. To refuse resources for an army was unthinkable - as unthinkable as placing them at the disposal of a king whom they did not trust, whom they suspected was a secret Catholic or at least a Catholic sympathiser, and who had made it perfectly clear that he considered a violent or military solution to his problems to be both attractive and justified. Nor was this a dilemma that could be left or put aside. Action was needed in Ireland and delay could be fatal.

Thus, in the months that followed, both king and opposition were being forced by the Irish rebellion to act in haste and both therefore took up more extreme positions than they otherwise might have done. On 8 November Pym succeeded in attaching the condition that the king should employ only 'such councillors as should be approved by parliament' to the offer of forces, and on 7 December Sir Arthur Haselrig moved that the army raised should be placed under the control of a general appointed by parliament. This proposal, known as the Militia Bill, involved a major encroachment on the king's established powers and prerogative which would not only be unacceptable to the king himself but also greatly offended many in the House of Commons. For those such as Edward Hyde, now the leader of a royalist party in parliament, who sought a settlement which would secure the rights and liberties of the subject within the existing structure, such radical measures would destroy the balance of the constitution and change the nature of government. They were therefore even more infuriated by the second part of Pym's tactics. Under the guise of a petition to the king he introduced the Grand Remonstrance, a statement of the grievances of parliament which recalled the abuses of the 1630s, reminded the MPs of what they had achieved by their unity thus far, and laid out the reforms which were still required. As a justification of the opposition campaign to rally parliament to their cause, it was skilful and effective. That it was passed in the Commons by the narrow margin of eleven votes is evidence of the difficulties faced by the opposition leaders at this stage. What ultimately outraged the king and his sympathisers was that on 22 November the decision was taken to publish the Remonstrance in an open appeal to the nation at large. In the eyes of cautious men this was not only an unprecedented insult to the king, it was also a dangerous incitement of popular opinion and an invitation to the people to involve themselves in what was rightly the business of the governing classes.

Charles's response to these provocations helped to polarise the political nation further. In December he rejected the Remonstrance out of hand. Evidence of popular displeasure at this was provided in the elections for the Mayor and Common Council of the City of London, which produced a large majority of opposition support. Charles tried to counter this, and in fact increased it, by appointing the brutal Sir Thomas Lunsford as Lieutenant of the Tower of London in an attempt to overawe the city. By the end of December it was clear that events were slipping beyond the control of either party. There was growing support in parliament and country for the king, as gentlemen of moderate and traditional outlook grew increasingly disturbed by the radicalism of the opposition. In late December the bishops were temporarily prevented from sitting in the House of Lords by popular demonstrations. When they demanded on their return that all proceedings in their absence be declared null and void, the lay lords rejected this as an infringement of their privileges. Convinced that his support was growing, and determined to act quickly to forestall any alliance of Lords and Commons over this matter, Charles attempted to seize the initiative. On 4 January 1642 he entered the House of Commons (in itself a breach of their privileges) to arrest five MPs - Pym, Haselrig, Hampden, Holles and Strode. Finding that they had been warned and escaped to safety in the city, the king declared that he intended nothing more than legal measures against them, an assurance rendered less than convincing by the fact that he was accompanied to the House by an escort of 400 armed men.

The attempt, and its failure, was a serious mistake. Suspicions that he was willing to use force to override opposition were confirmed, his apparent lack of respect for his subjects' rights and liberties was reinforced, and many waverers were confirmed in their belief that the measures taken by the opposition were necessary. Popular demonstrations in London increased, and were probably only partly orchestrated by Pym and his allies. Isolated, and possibly afraid of mob violence against his family, the king left London on 10 January. According to John Morrill, this was probably another serious misjudgement. The opposition control of the Commons was by no means secure, and if Charles had remained in London to rally his sympathisers they might yet have swung the House in his favour. As it was, they had to demonstrate their loyalty by leaving it. Morrill argues that 'One of the striking things about parliamentary divisions in the months after the Attempt on the Five Members and ... the royal retreat from London is the way Pym's majority remained constant in a rapidly dwindling House. If half of those who had voted against the Grand Remonstrance, and who subsequently abandoned London with the king, had stayed put, it is unlikely that any of the major escalations towards war could have been put through the House of Commons'. As it was, Pym had a free hand. Utilising the king's isolation and unpopularity, he pushed through the Clerical Disabilities Act, which excluded the bishops from the House of Lords, and transformed the uncompleted Militia Bill into an Ordinance, which did not require the king's assent. It was approved by a depleted House of Lords in February 1642.

Thereafter, it is difficult to envisage any peaceful outcome of the struggle, although it was not until August that the king formally embarked on war by raising his standard at Nottingham. The descent into civil war was slow, piecemeal, and often reluctant, quite in accordance with Whitelocke's bemused claim that it was unsought and unplanned (see page 27). The spring and early summer saw a jockeying for political and military advantage, as both sides tried to secure their position, but many of the military preparations were essentially defensive in character, as if both parties were reluctant to take any initiative that might remove lingering hopes of settlement. There is little doubt that the king's removal from London to York increased the opposition's fear of attack. It is significant that it was in January 1642 that they took steps to ensure that the great royal arsenal kept in Hull was under the control of a governor nominated by parliament, Sir John Hotham. In April the king attempted to gain control of Hull, and was denied entry by Sir John. It is interesting, in the light of Hotham's later attempt to change sides, that he refused to give up the arms without a warrant from both king and parliament. In a confused and difficult situation Hotham's actions may well have represented, not so much committed support for parliament, as a refusal to take sides at all. He simply stuck rigidly to what he perceived as his duty. By declaring him a traitor for his actions and refusing to withdraw this when parliament took responsibility in Hotham's defence, Charles ultimately made Hotham's decision for him.

A propaganda battle followed in which both sides sought to justify their actions in the light of aggression by the other. Parliament sent out orders for the raising of the militia and the king issued commissions of array in June - the unfortunate magistrates who received these orders were thereby forced to decide which, if either, to obey. A series of skirmishes took place in different counties as the committed supporters tried to secure the area and its administration for their party. In a final attempt at settlement, parliament presented the king with the Nineteen Propositions (see Appendix) but since these included parliamentary control of the militia, restrictions on the king's choice of advisers and reform of the Church by a national synod (assembly of ministers), they can hardly have expected that he would find them acceptable. It is more likely that the propositions represented the minimum safeguards that the opposition leaders felt that they required. Charles's reply was a masterly statement of the royalist case, in which he firmly claimed the moral and legal high ground; arguing that England already had a balanced constitution and that the powers of parliament were sufficient to prevent 'the evil of absolute monarchy ... which is tyranny' he claimed that further change would spark off a worse evil, an uprising of the common people.

Conrad Russell has raised questions about the reasons why there was so little serious negotiation in the spring and summer of 1642, suggesting that the possibility of a Scottish alliance distracted both sides from the recognition that they had to find some solution for their difficulties. While this is a possibility, it seems more likely that the crucial factor was the endemic lack of trust between the parties. It is impossible to believe that, by this stage, either side could have faith in the promises of the other, and the propaganda battle of the spring had undoubtedly deepened mutual suspicions. John Morrill has also drawn attention to the growing anarchy in the provinces, created by a weakness if not a breakdown of normal administration coupled with an increasing intensity of popular feeling. This, he points out, has been thoroughly documented by Anthony Fletcher in his *Outbreak of the Civil War*. Morrill continues, 'The civil war may not have begun as a collapse of government in the provinces, but I would argue that fear of and belief in an imminent collapse into anarchy was a far more important conditioner of the Junto's responses to developments in high politics than was looking kindly on Scottish demands, certainly after the parliamentary recess of 1641'. What is clear from this confused picture is that the war was indeed unplanned; the most logical explanation of the actions of both parties in the early months of 1642 is that in both cases they believed that they were the victims of the other's actual or intended aggression, and in both cases, they ultimately took up arms in their own defence.

6 Conclusion - From Crisis to Conflict

In 1640 the monarchy and the system of government in England was in crisis because the governing class on whom the king relied was offended by the actions and practices that he had adopted since his accession in 1625. Faced with long-term difficulties in finance, in the need to govern three different kingdoms (each with its own culture and traditions) and, above all, by religious divisions which cut across these national boundaries, Charles's attempts to find solutions which accorded with his own political and religious convictions had succeeded only in alienating the majority of his subjects. With hindsight it is possible to see that a genuine compromise was always unlikely, because the king did not believe it to be necessary. His belief in the divine authority that he held, and in the forms of government that he was establishing in Church and State, was unshakeable, and although he could be forced into concessions (as he was in 1640 and 1641) it was always clear that he regarded these as temporary and felt no obligation to maintain them any longer than he was forced to. When he did listen to the advice of his more moderate and astute councillors, for example in calling parliament in 1628 and again in 1640, he found it impossible to establish a compromise which did not offend his own deepest convictions. As a result, the attempt by the opposition in parliament to use their financial power to bring him to a settlement was doomed to failure, because without his sincere commitment to uphold any agreement, there was no point at which they could feel secure in the gains that had been made. Essentially, the king saw them as rebels and, if restored to the free exercise of his powers, would be likely to treat them as such. To that extent the possibility of a military outcome to the crisis had always existed. The king was willing to use force to solve his problems because, in his view, he had the right to do so; what he lacked in 1640-1 was the means. Thus, the first steps toward civil war were taken in the summer and autumn of 1641 when the emergence of a royalist party within parliament made it possible for the king to fight. In that sense, the doubtful legality of Strafford's execution, the constitutional issues raised by further attempts to limit the king's power, and particularly the religious issues raised by the desire to reform the Church, were all causes of the war, since they contributed greatly to the development of a royalist party.

This revival in the king's fortunes created fear and tension in the ranks of the opposition, but it did not necessarily lead to civil war. The reluctance with which military measures were put into effect in 1642 indicates that both sides would have continued to seek political victory if given the time to engineer it. The leaders of the royalist party, such as Edward Hyde, were pursuing a compromise settlement, not the reversal of all that had been done since November 1640. What deprived the participants of the time to achieve any of these goals was the outbreak of rebellion in Ireland. Not only did it drive fear and tension to new heights by raising the spectre of popery, it also created a problem that demanded an immediate, military solution. By bringing the power struggle into the open, it polarised the parties and by introducing a note of urgency it made a rapid resolution of the issues necessary. As a result, both sides took extreme actions - the publication of the Grand Remonstrance was an appeal to the people against the king, the attempt to arrest the Five Members an attack on the privileges of parliament and the lives and liberties of its members. Moreover, by raising a military problem, the rebellion increased the likelihood of a military solution. Once forces began to be raised the question of whom they would be used against was raised with them. In the end, men took up arms because they feared that, if they did not, they would be the victims of armed attack by others. 'I am not for a tame resignation of our religion, lives and liberties into the hands of our adversaries who seek to devour it', declared Whitelocke in 1642; and in the end it seemed, to both sides, that the only course of action open to them was to fight.

Making notes on 'From Crisis to Conflict'

(N.B. for general advice on effective note-making, see the Preface).
Explaining why the crisis of 1640 became the war of 1642 involves the examination of a series of actions and errors on the part of king and parliament, and of a sequence of events which led them to war. In other words, in order to understand why war occurred we have to establish how it came about. You will therefore need to make detailed notes which trace this sequence from November 1640 to August 1642. At the same time, the chapter also seeks to analyse certain issues in greater depth, and it may simplify your task if you make notes on these aspects of the period separately. It is therefore suggested that you:
1. Read through the entire chapter first;
2. Re-read and make notes based on the sub-headings provided in the chapter. The bulk of these notes should provide a sequential outline of events, in which you can signify key developments in two areas - the growth of mutual fear and distrust, and the gradual loss of unity in parliament. These notes will be drawn from sections 2a, b, c, 3, 4a, c, d, 5 and 6.
3. In addition you should make separate notes on certain key issues which are analysed in greater depth; (a) the nature of the opposition (section 2d); (b) religious issues (section 4b); (c) the nature of

royalism (section 4c).

You will be able to make these notes as you work through the chapter, but it will be useful for you to use separate sheets of paper so that you can extract or slot them in as separate units.

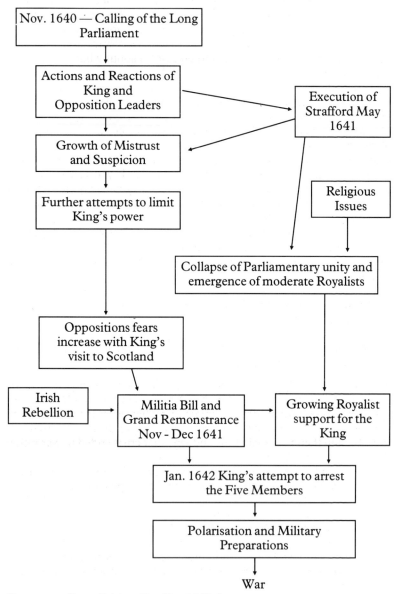

Summary - From Crisis to Conflict, 1640-2

Answering essay questions on 'From Crisis to Conflict'

Most examination questions about this period focus on the central question of why civil war occurred in 1642. They may be phrased or presented in different ways, but they are essentially concerned with the same issue. It is therefore possible to prepare for a range of essay questions by defining certain themes or factors as central to the issue of why war broke out. As you read and take notes about what happened in the build-up to war, you are presented with a mass of events, individual actions, beliefs and attitudes, which contributed to the outcome; in order to make sense of what was happening, these elements need to be grouped around common themes such as religion or politics, or arranged in sequence to show a process taking place, such as the growth of mistrust or the collapse of parliamentary unity. These themes and processes then constitute the factors, both long and short-term, which can be said to have combined to cause the war. If you can explain the existence and impact of these key causal factors, you will be able to write a good response to almost any examination question on the reasons for the outbreak of war in 1642.

The first stage is to identify the main causal factors outlined in the material that you have studied. To do this, you should use your notes on *From Crisis to Conflict*, in conjunction with the outline of events provided in Chapter 1.

1. Compile a list of the main causal factors leading to
   (a) the crisis of 1640,
   (b) the war of 1642.
2. For each factor, write a brief description of what happened and how this led to crisis and/or war.

You are now in a position to plan and write an essay response to the question, 'Why did civil war break out in England in 1642?' The best approach would probably be to explain first what issues led to discontent and the crisis that came to a head with the calling of the Long Parliament in 1640, and then to explain how and why that crisis ended in war rather than an agreed settlement.

The second stage is to consider how this material might be applied to a range of different questions. Consider the list of questions below.

1. Why did the crisis of 1640 lead to civil war in 1642?
2. Was the Civil War of 1642 inevitable?
3. How far was the English Civil War of 1642 the result of long-term problems within the system of government?
4. How far was Charles I responsible for the outbreak of civil war in 1642?

5. 'It was religion that drove men to war in 1642.' How far do you agree?
6. Why were so many MPs prepared to go to war against the king in 1642?
7. Why did king and parliament take up arms in 1642?

Each question lays stress on a different aspect of why war occurred, and essay responses to them should do the same, but that aspect must always be assessed alongside other causal factors, as the words 'how far?' often indicate. Thus, while each response will draw upon similar historical knowledge and content, the question dictates how that knowledge is used. Questions 1, 2 and 3 require you to compare the underlying causes of the crisis with the actions and errors of the king and parliament in trying to deal with it, and decide which were more important in causing the war. Questions 4 and 5 focus on one particular causal factor, and require you to explain the part played by that factor and then compare it with the contribution made by the other factors that you have defined, while questions 6 and 7 ask you to use the factors to explain the actions of king and parliament. In each case the question dictates a starting point, and the nature of your overall conclusion, but a full response will require you to call on and utilise all the main causal factors that you have identified and defined in stage one above.

Answering source-based questions on 'From Crisis to Conflict'

Handling source-based questions successfully requires the application of particular skills which need to be acquired and practised. The basic techniques begin with comprehension of the meaning of given sources, which may not be entirely straightforward given the problems of seventeenth-century language and expression. Sources therefore need to be read carefully, and the sense of unfamiliar words or usage can often be deduced from the context in which they appear. Perhaps more important, sources are rarely written for the purposes for which historians seek to use them. They are often fragmented, and may well include obscure references to people and events of the time. Thus they cannot merely be read as processed information, but require interpretation, using knowledge of the period and the context in which they were produced, as well as evidence and clues contained within them. You should bear this in mind as you attempt to answer the following questions.

1 The Causes of Conflict
Read the comments made by Slingsby and Baxter on page 28 regarding parliamentary grievances in 1640. Answer the following questions.
a) What were the main grievances outlined in the two sources?
   (2 marks)

b) In what ways do the two accounts differ? (2 marks)
c) Explain the reasons for these differences. (4 marks)
    Now read the comments of Slingsby and Whitelocke about the
    attitudes and expectations of MPs in 1640, given on page 27, and
    Clarendon's account of his conversation with Pym, given on
    page 31.
d) How can you reconcile Slingsby's optimistic expectations with his
    account of parliamentary grievances? (2 marks)
e) In what ways did his attitude differ from that of Pym? (2 marks)
f) How reliable is Clarendon's interpretation of Pym's comments likely
    to be? Explain your answer. (4 marks)
g) Given your knowledge of the period and its attitudes, what do you
    think Pym meant by 'removing all grievances and pulling up the
    causes of them by the roots'? (4 marks)
h) Treating these five sources as a set, and interpreting them in the light
    of your knowledge of the period, explain what they suggest about
    why civil war broke out in 1642. (15 marks)

2 The Role of Religion
Read Digby and Slingsby's comments on religious issues, given on pages
43 and 44-5, and Baxter's comments on the Irish rebellion on page 52.
Answer the following questions.
a) Given that Digby suggests widespread agreement on the issue, what
    do you think he had in mind as a 'Reformation of Church
    government'? (2 marks)
b) In what ways did MPs' attitudes on this issue differ? (3 marks)
c) What reasons does Slingsby give for favouring the retention of
    bishops in the Church? (2 marks)
d) Do you consider him to be motivated by religious, political or social
    considerations? Explain your answer. (4 marks)
e) According to Baxter, the Irish Rebellion had an enormous impact on
    people's attitudes to the king. Use your knowledge of the period to
    explain i) what he means by this claim, and ii) how far his evidence
    can be trusted on this issue? (9 marks)
f) Collectively, these sources suggest that religious concerns and their
    impact varied from one person to another. Using your knowledge of
    the period to help you interpret the sources, explain what they
    indicate about the different types of religious grievances that existed
    and in what ways religion helped to cause civil war. (15 marks)

CHAPTER 4

A Nation Divided, 1642-3

1 The Process of Division

Although the official outbreak of the Civil War dates from August 1642, when the king raised his standard at Nottingham and called for volunteers, the process of division and the search for strategic advantage had begun some months before that, and continued for many months thereafter. In January 1642 the king left London. In February Henrietta Maria sailed for Holland to raise men and money for the king. In April the king was denied access to the arms in Hull by the parliamentarian governor, Sir John Hotham, and while the ensuing propaganda war raged between king and parliament, the weapons were hastily transferred to London. In June, while the Nineteen Propositions were theoretically still under discussion, both sides sent out orders to their county commissioners for the raising of troops. In July the navy declared for parliament and the Earl of Warwick was appointed Admiral, the king appointed the Marquess of Hertford as Lieutenant-General of his western armies, and the Earl of Essex was chosen for overall command of the parliamentary forces. In this context, the call for volunteers to Nottingham was only one more step, and not the final one, in the military division of the country.

It is difficult to piece together a coherent account of the early months of the war, since it consisted for the most part of military skirmishes designed to secure local or regional control. In August and September 1642 both sides were engaged in assembling volunteers and in securing strong points. Portsmouth, for example, was declared to be for the king by its governor, George Goring, in August but was captured for parliament by Sir William Waller in early September. A similar struggle was waged for Sherborne Castle. Here the Marquess of Hertford was besieged by parliamentarians until Sir Ralph Hopton was driven to join him after being defeated near Yeovil. With this extra strength, the royalists were able to hold the castle until they chose to evacuate it, Hertford leaving to organise recruits in South Wales and Hopton to secure Cornwall for the king. By December the struggle had resolved itself into four main theatres in which the protagonists were occupied for the winter and early spring. In the east and south-east the strength of parliamentarian feeling and the proximity of London allowed parliament's supporters to secure control, and to organise associations of counties (such as the Eastern Association) for military and administrative purposes. In the west, the midlands and the north, the outcome was more finely balanced.

However, in all areas the conduct of the war was characterised by a marked reluctance by many to participate. Between June and October many county communities concluded local agreements to cease recruiting and prevent bloodshed within their own counties. Some went further, and, as in the Treaty of Bunbury drawn up in Cheshire in December 1642, agreed to raise a local force to prevent others fighting within their county boundaries. Some truces seem to have been part of a local conflict in which both sides sought a breathing-space, as in Devon in February 1643, but others represented genuine efforts to end or prevent war. From all parts of the country, accommodation petitions were sent to both king and parliament, begging them to resolve their differences by peaceful agreement. Throughout the winter and spring of 1642-3, until after the failure of the Oxford negotiations in May 1643, hopes of peace or a short-lived war survived to delay and complicate the process of division and the nature of military manoeuvres.

Already, however, parliament had come close to disaster, when the king attempted to resolve the whole issue by capturing London itself. In August he was joined at Nottingham by his nephews, Prince Rupert and Prince Maurice, who were experienced soldiers from the United Provinces (Holland). Thereafter he moved west to Shrewsbury to join up with his Welsh supporters and began a march towards the capital. Intercepted by parliament's main forces under the Earl of Essex, who had been based at Worcester, he fought an indecisive battle at Edgehill. Although the royalist cavalry were victorious in routing their opponents, their inability to regroup and rejoin the battle allowed the parliamentarian foot to retreat in good order. While the battle itself produced no clear-cut result, Essex's withdrawal to Warwick at the end of the day left the king's road to London clear, and Banbury and Oxford were both occupied by the royalists while Rupert stormed the town of Brentford. Only when Essex joined up with the London Trained Bands under Major-General Philip Skippon at Turnham Green on 13 November were the royalist forces held, and forced to retreat into winter quarters at Oxford. The campaign had shown the extent of early advantage held by the king. Unlike the parliament he had a clear target to aim at (London) and hence a clear strategy. Able to draw on experienced cavalry among his supporters, he had defeated parliament's untried forces, and had Rupert's cavalry been as strong in discipline and tactics as they were in attack, Edgehill might have been an outright and decisive victory for the king. Although not apparent at the time, the Edgehill campaign and a quick victory was probably the king's best chance of a successful outcome to the war.

Without such a rapid resolution of the conflict, the war now settled into a series of regional campaigns as both sides sought to secure their territorial base. This was important as a source not only of strategic advantage, but also of supplies of men and money. In the north the Earl of Newcastle was appointed commander of the king's forces and entered Yorkshire in early December to confront the local forces raised by the Fairfaxes. Although Fairfax was successful in the West Riding, York was held for the king, and in February 1643 the queen arrived there with arms brought from Holland via Bridlington. In June 1643 Newcastle inflicted a heavy defeat on the Fairfaxes at Adwalton Moor, forcing them to retreat into Hull which was the only stronghold in Yorkshire left in parliamentarian hands. Meanwhile, the struggle in the west had been finely balanced, with Hopton and the royalists secure in the south-west and Waller's parliamentarian forces achieving significant successes in South Wales, Somerset and Gloucestershire. In July 1643 a parliamentarian victory at Lansdown near Bath was negated by the defeat of Waller at Roundway Down near Devizes. In the same month, Prince Rupert successfully stormed the parliamentarian stronghold of Bristol, giving the royalist cause the advantage in the west. However, the success of the parliamentarian cavalry led by Oliver Cromwell in the eastern counties allowed parliament's forces to relieve Gainsborough in the east and extend their effective control north into Lincolnshire.

The late spring of 1643, therefore, produced no military outcome to the war, although the advantage lay with the royalists at that point. What was more important at this stage was that the struggle was clearly going to be prolonged, and any hopes of peace or neutrality entertained by those who were torn between, or uncommitted to, the warring parties were clearly shown to be illusory. To confirm this, the failure of negotiations that took place in Oxford during April and May 1643 showed how far apart the objectives of the two sides remained. In the words of Derek Hirst in his study of *Authority and Conflict, 1603-58*

1 The spring of 1643, so agonising for those at Westminster and their supporters, was a watershed for the country. Despite the fulminations of king and parliament, neutralism had until now been a perfectly logical response to the war. Did not both sides
5 protest their devotion to the same ideals in church and state? But the failure of new negotiations at Oxford that spring ... showed that whatever their rhetoric the two sides were far apart. There was now no escaping the conclusion that civil war had to be fought out.

Thus it can be claimed that the spring of 1643 was the end of the beginning. Then, and only then, did it become valid to speak of a divided nation, and to consider and examine the causes and nature of that division.

2 The Nature of Division

a) Beliefs and Motivation

In the autumn of 1642 the country faced the stark reality of civil war and slowly began to take sides. The nature of division and the patterns of allegiance that emerged are described by contemporary observers from both sides with a surprising degree of unanimity.

According to Clarendon,

1 Training as volunteers for parliament began to be practised in
many places of the kingdom; but only in those corporations
[towns] and by those inferior people who were notorious for
faction and schism in religion [schism means division, and
5 Clarendon is probably referring to those who refused to accept the
Anglican Church as it was - the puritans. He may also have had in
mind those who had gone a step further, and left the Church to
worship in private meetings - puritan separatists, although they
were relatively few in number at this stage]. The people generally
10 (except in great towns and corporations where, beside the natural
malignity [resentment], the factious lecturers and emissaries from
parliament had poisoned the affections) and especially those of
quality, were loyally inclined ... [In the West] most of the gentry
were engaged against [the parliament] as they were in truth
15 throughout the kingdom; yet the common people, especially in the
clothing parts of Somersetshire, were generally too much inclined
to them ... [In Somerset the parliamentarian leaders were] for the
most part clothiers ... though the gentlemen of ancient families and
estates in that country were, for the most part, well-affected to the
20 king ... [In Gloucestershire it was] the yeomanry who had been
most forward and seditious, being very wealthy ... In Lancashire
men of no name ... [and] the town of Manchester (out of factious
humour and pride of their wealth) opposed the king. [In
Yorkshire] besides the Lord Fairfax, there were in truth few of
25 good reputation and fortune who ran that way ... Leeds, Halifax
and Bradford (three very populous and rich towns which,
depending wholly upon clothiers, naturally maligned the gentry)
were wholly at their disposition...

Clarendon's analysis reveals something of the geographical division of
the kingdom, for he deals mainly with the northern and western areas
that came under royalist control, but emphasises much more strongly
the class divisions which characterised the two sides. It is necessary to
allow for some exaggeration in this matter, for to the seventeenth-
century mind the loyalty and support of the gentry, the governing and
social elite, would be of greatest value, and help to vindicate the cause
for which they fought. Quite literally, these supporters represented the
best of society. In this case, however, Clarendon's account is borne out
by those of parliamentarian supporters such as Richard Baxter and
Thomas May. According to Baxter,

1 A great part of the Lords forsook the parliament, and so did many
of the House of Commons, and came to the king; but that was after
Edgehill fight [October 1642] when the king was at Oxford. A very

great part of the knights and gentlemen ... adhered to the king;
5 except in Middlesex, Essex, Suffolk, Norfolk, Cambridgeshire
etc., where the king with his army never came. And could he have
got footing there, it is like that it would have been there as it was in
other places. And most of the tenants of these gentlemen and also
most of the poorest of the people, whom the other called 'the
10 rabble' did follow the gentry and were for the king. On the
parliament's side were (besides themselves) some of the gentry in
most counties, and the greatest part of the tradesmen and
freeholders, and the middle sort of men, especially in those
corporations and countries which depend on clothing and such
15 manufactures.

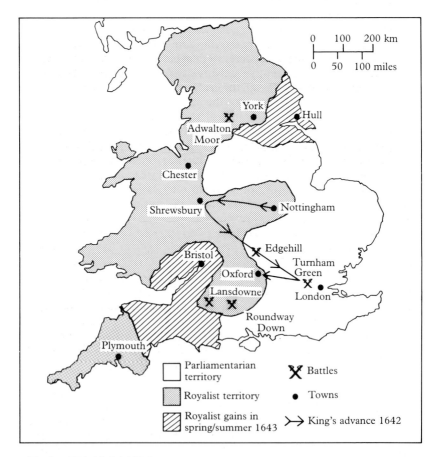

England Divided 1642-3

There seems little doubt, therefore, that parliament drew much support from the middle ranks of society, particularly in the urban and manufacturing areas. Examples of volunteers from these socio-economic groups can be found all over the country, but particularly in the clothing areas of West Yorkshire, Somerset and Gloucestershire. The urban support for the cause is evidenced by the role played by key urban centres in holding up the royalist advance on London in 1643. Bristol was captured after a short siege, but Plymouth, Gloucester and Hull withstood the royalist attacks. Nor, in Baxter's eyes, was there any uncertainty about the reason for this.

> 1 If you ask the reasons of this [he continued] ask also why in France
>   it is not commonly the nobility nor the beggars, but the merchants
>   and middle sort of men that [are] Protestants. The reasons which
>   the party themselves gave was because (say they) the tradesmen
> 5 have a correspondency with London, and so are grown to be a far
>   more intelligent sort of men than the ignorant peasants ... And the
>   freeholders (say they) were not enslaved to their landlords as
>   the tenants are. The gentry (say they) are wholly, by their estates
>   and ambition, more dependent on the king than their tenants on
> 10 them ...

Thus he attributes greater economic and intellectual independence to the yeomanry and urban craftsmen than to those above or below them in the social scale, reinforcing the importance of social class. Where Clarendon attributed the attitude of the less substantial gentry and the middling-sort to envy or 'malignancy' towards their betters, Baxter points to the fear of upheaval and desire to preserve their power and possessions that motivated many supporters of the king. Again, there is other evidence to bear this out. Fear of disorder was a powerful motive among royalists as their 'party' took shape in 1641-2, and complaints about the breakdown of censorship, of radical preachers undermining the control exercised by the church, of public demonstrations and even enclosure riots were common throughout that year. It was no coincidence that the king's most effective propaganda came in his reply to the Nineteen Propositions when he argued that further changes in the constitution would 'destroy all rights and proprieties [property], all distinctions of families and merit, and by this means this splendid and excellently distinguished form of government [would] end in a dark, equal chaos of confusion'.

If class interest or ambition was one reason for the choosing of sides, another was religion. Clarendon referred to the 'factious' spirit among some urban corporations and the 'lecturers' that he mentions were the puritan preachers employed by many towns to hold week-day sermons, until this was forbidden by Laud. Baxter's conviction that religion was a decisive motivation is even stronger.

1 Though it must be confessed that the public safety and liberty
wrought very much with most, especially with the nobility and
gentry who adhered to the parliament; yet it was principally the
differences about religious matters that filled up the parliament's
5 armies, and put the resolution and valour into their soldiers ... Not
that the matter of Bishops or no Bishops was the main thing ... but
the generality of the people through the land ... who were then
called Puritans, ... religious persons that used to talk of God and
Heaven and Scripture and holiness, and to follow sermons ... and
10 speak against swearing, cursing, drunkenness etc: I say the main
body of this sort of men, both preachers and people, adhered to the
parliament. And on the other side, the gentry that ... went to
Church and heard Common Prayer ... and spoke against this
strictness and preciseness in religion ... the main body of these
were against the parliament.

Again there is a great deal of evidence to support these contentions.
Example after example could be cited of puritan volunteers for
parliament, of parliamentarian troops destroying hated symbols of the
Laudian régime like altar rails and surplices, of regiments listening to
sermons and singing psalms in battle. Not all of these were of the
'middling-sort', but a significant proportion of the volunteers seem to
have fitted this description. One such example is provided by Nehemiah
Wharton, a sergeant in Lord Essex's army, who wrote to his master, Mr
Willingham (indicating that Wharton had been apprenticed or
employed by Willingham and therefore fits the 'middling' social
category):

1 Wednesday: Mr Love gave us a famous sermon this day. Also, the
soldiers brought the holy [altar] rails from Chiswick and burned
them in our town. Thursday: I marched towards Uxbridge. And at
Hillingdon, one mile from Uxbridge, the rails being gone, we got
5 the surplice to make us handkerchiefs; and one of the soldiers wore
it to Uxbridge.

Religious motivation, however, spread through all classes. Describing
the situation in Nottinghamshire, Lucy Hutchinson declared that 'the
popish gentry were wholly for the king' while the puritan Hutchinsons
adhered to the parliamentary cause. Their cousin,

1 Mr Henry Ireton ... having had an education in the strictest way of
godliness ... was the chief promoter of the parliament's interest in
the county. But finding it generally disaffected, all he could do
when the king approached it was to gather a troop of those godly
5 people which the cavaliers drove out, and with them go into the
army of my lord of Essex.

At the opposite end of the scale, Clarendon describes the intense royalist feeling among the common people of Cornwall (despite 'a wonderful and superstitious reverence towards the name of a parliament') because of their 'full submission and love of the established government of Church and State, especially to that part of the Church as concerned the liturgy, or Book of Common Prayer, which was a most general object of veneration [respect] with the people'. In some cases, puritan destruction of decorations and statues in local churches caused great resentment, and the parliamentarian Thomas May remarked that 'some who were not bad men [were concerned about] the extreme licence which the common people ... took to themselves of reforming without authority, order or decency ... To this were added those daily reports of ridiculous conventicles [meetings] and preachings made by tradesmen and illiterate people of the lowest rank, to the scandal and offence of many'.

It could be said, therefore, that as Whig and Marxist historians argued, England divided in 1642 on the basis of concerns about political liberty, religious conviction, and class interest, with a remarkable compatibility between these apparently diverse motives. The strong links between middling and urban social groups and puritan convictions, and between respect for the authority of King and Church and fear of social disorder, meant that belief and conviction often coincided with personal and material interests. Both the central leadership whose commitments were made in parliament during 1641 and 1642 and the provincial supporters whose response emerged in the autumn of 1642 shared these common motivations.

b) Cross-currents and Complexities

A closer examination of the evidence, however, indicates that such generalisations are far too simplistic. Baxter and Clarendon might agree on the broad social division of support, but both indicate that members of the gentry did support the parliamentary cause. Numerous individuals fail to conform to the stereotypes drawn above. In Derbyshire, the mainstay of the parliamentary cause was Sir John Gell, a great supporter of the Ship Money tax described by Lucy Hutchinson as 'a foul adulterer ... and so unjust that without any remorse he suffered his men indifferently to plunder both honest men and cavaliers'. In his *History of the Parliament*, Thomas May describes the patterns of allegiance in terms which broadly agree with Clarendon and Baxter, but which also reveal some of the complex processes which went into the making of those patterns.

1 In Suffolk, Norfolk, Cambridgeshire, Essex, Herts. Hunts. there was as much unanimity of opinion and affection in those counties

... as was to be found in any part of England; but it was especially
among the common people. For a great ... number of the gentry,
5 and those of highest rank among them, were disaffected to the
parliament ... Which might have thrown those counties (if not
wholly carried them to the other side) into as much distraction and
sad calamity as any other part of the land had felt ... if those
gentlemen had not been curbed and suppressed by that timely care
10 which the parliament took, and more particularly by the successful
services of one gentleman, Mr Oliver Cromwell of Huntingdon. In
the south-western counties [the Marquess of Hertford and Sir
Ralph Hopton, commanding for the king] were both opposed ... by
private gentlemen of those counties.

What May indicates, and this can also be seen in the accounts by
Clarendon and Baxter, is that divisions cut across most counties. Thus
before the loyalty of the area was defined, an internal struggle occurred,
and the outcome could be dictated by the actions of particular
individuals and the influence of local or regional factors. In the
south-eastern counties within the proximity of London, parliament
undoubtedly strengthened their cause, and as Baxter noted, the king
never came there to help or stir up his sympathisers. Even so, the relative
ease with which parliament gained control of the area owed much to the
individual efforts of Cromwell. In the south-west and in Nottinghamshire the parliamentarian gentry were in a minority, and like Henry
Ireton, could do little but surrender control of their county and move on
to serve their cause elsewhere. As Lucy Hutchinson described it,

1 Before the flame of the war broke out in the top of the chimneys,
the smoke ascended in every country ... [and] in many places there
were fierce contests and disputes (almost to blood) even at the first;
for in the progress every county had the civil war (more or less)
5 within itself.

This evidence reveals the division of the nation as a gradual, piecemeal
process, beginning before the official outbreak of hostilities and
continuing for some months thereafter. Hence the local and regional
struggles, which, with the exception of the Edgehill campaign,
pre-occupied both sides in the winter of 1642-3. It is, moreover,
increasingly clear that these struggles were essentially the work of
committed minorities rather than the county community as a whole.
The difficulty of generalising about gentry reactions and motivations is
illustrated by Lawrence Stone in *The Causes of the English Revolution,
1529-1642*:

1 Despite the prodigious amount of research devoted to the subject
in recent years, the motives for the alignments of the gentry when

the war began are still not wholly clear ... [Socio-economic theories based on 'rising gentry', 'mere gentry', and 'declining gentry' have not proved convincing in the light of the evidence]. Far more decisive than any socio-economic correlations is that with religion. In Yorkshire over one third of the Royalist gentry were Catholics, and over half of the Parliamentarians were Puritan ... All the Parliamentary leaders in Yorkshire had a previous record of strong Puritan sympathies. There is reason to think that those who had opposed the Crown on purely constitutional and political grounds in the 1620s and 1630s tended to swing back to the King with Sir Edward Hyde [Clarendon] in 1642, while those who had also opposed the Crown on religious grounds were far more likely to stick to Pym and fight for the Parliamentary cause.

What Stone shows is that religion can account for the allegiance of something approaching half of the gentry and that it can explain the behaviour of those who were most clearly and actively committed. Yet if over half of the parliamentarian gentry in Yorkshire were puritans, that still leaves a significant minority to be accounted for. Not all counties divided on such clear religious lines. If fear of social upheaval helps to explain why others chose the royalist cause, we are still left with a substantial group of participants among the gentry whose motives must have arisen from political considerations, or else from other personal, local or random concerns.

While political and religious motives remain significant and valid as broad generalisations, the extent to which they controlled or influenced individual actions becomes rather more questionable. Geography, the prevailing political interest of the locality and the needs of survival must be taken into account. In Lancashire the royalists quickly laid siege to parliamentarian Manchester and Bolton, and forcibly conscripted local men to fight with them. The puritan minister Adam Martindale describes how his brother tried to avoid the fighting until, faced with the threat of being rounded up and marched off by the royalists, he went to Bolton and volunteered for the defence of the town. Thus some men were forced to take one side, or pressurised to volunteer for the other. Few went as far in trying to protect their lands and fortunes as the Earl of Kingston who, according to Lucy Hutchinson, 'divided his sons between both parties and concealed himself' until he was forced to make a choice, but it is difficult to sustain the view that all, or even the majority, of those who fought made a conscious choice based on principle and belief as to which side to support.

There are, moreover, many examples of men for whom conscience and principle did not dictate a clear path to one side or another. Throughout the spring and summer of 1642 petitions poured in to king and parliament from all parts of the country, almost universally demanding that they compose their differences. Government by

King-in-Parliament was the ideal of the constitution, and government by the king under the law was the desire of many who fought on both sides. A clear example of these uncertainties and of the difficulties that they created is afforded by Sir John Hotham, whose actions in securing Hull for the parliament were of crucial importance in the outcome of the war. Not only did this deny the king arms for 16,000 men, possession of the major supply port in the north of England and access to continental aid, but as a parliamentarian stronghold, Hull afforded refuge to the Fairfaxes in June 1643 and forced the Earl of Newcastle to delay his march south to join the king.

Yet Hotham's actions could more accurately be described as reactions, and were certainly not the result of a coherent commitment and careful decision-making. In 1640-2 he supported the parliamentary opposition because he disapproved of the king's high-handed actions, and because he was personally at odds with his monarch. He had opposed the collection of Ship Money and the billetting of soldiers in Yorkshire during the Bishops' Wars, and Charles had responded by insulting him and passing him over for appointment as governor of Hull. In January 1642 Hotham therefore accepted the nomination of parliament for the post, and seems to have been genuinely seeking to do his duty in this capacity when he refused the king access to the town and arsenal in April of that year. Finding himself declared a traitor, he had little choice but to appeal to parliament for vindication, and to espouse its cause. Thereafter he clearly had second thoughts and came close to surrendering the town in July 1642. In the winter of 1642-3 he quarrelled with the corporation, and made clear his dislike of the puritan influence among the Aldermen. Greatly concerned by the threat of popular disorder, he also became disillusioned with the parliamentary campaign, especially when the Fairfaxes were chosen to command the parliamentary forces rather than himself and his son. What finally tipped the balance seems to have been the Oxford negotiations; he blamed their failure upon the excessive demands of parliament. Thus in June 1643 Hotham agreed to hand Hull over to the royalists, but was prevented by the vigilance of the corporation. Instead he was arrested and sent to London, where both he and Captain Hotham were executed as traitors in 1644. Hotham's case reveals the dilemmas facing those of moderate beliefs, the narrow margins that could separate royalist from parliamentarian, the personal or random elements that could dictate their final decisions, and the momentous influence that such factors could have on the outcome of events.

The complexities outlined above have been emphasised in recent local studies and the work of John Morrill, whose *Revolt of the Provinces* investigated the patchwork of responses that characterised the outbreak of war. What such studies also revealed was the importance of two other considerations in influencing the attitude of county communities to the growing conflict - the twin factors of neutralism and localism.

c) The Influence of Neutralism

In 1642 every man was faced with a choice of sides - and many opted to choose no side at all. In the words of Clarendon, 'the number of these who desired to sit still was greater than of those who desired to engage in either party'. In Staffordshire the justices met to declare their county a neutral zone, in Cheshire and Yorkshire the royalist commissioners of array and the parliamentary militia commissioners (those who had been given the task of raising troops) made a mutual agreement not to proceed with their work in those counties. In Lincolnshire the gentry declared that they would not fight for or against the king, and raised a cavalry troop 'for the preservation of peace within themselves' and the defence of the county. In towns and boroughs the picture was much the same. Leicester shut its gates to all 'foreigners' and when the Earl of Bath came to South Molton in Devon to raise forces for the king, 'the common sort of the town fell in a great rage with the mayor and his company for giving licence that they should enter' and refused to allow the gentlemen to read their commission. Eventually they were attacked by the crowd 'some with muskets loaden, some with halberds and black bills [spears and axes], some with clubs ... The women had filled all the steps of the cross with great stones, and got up and sat on them, swearing if they did come there they would brain them'. The commissioners beat a hasty retreat from the town.

Nor were these reactions in any way uncommon. In investigating this issue, John Morrill found attempted neutrality pacts in twenty-two English counties. As he described it 'Fear [of disorder] drove some men into royalism; it drove far more into neutralism. Faced by the threat of social disintegration ... most counties closed ranks behind county barriers, determined (as they had been in the 1630s) to protect the administrative integrity of their shires as the first line of defence against disorder.' These pacts fell into two broad categories. The first consists of pacts made between the royalist commissioners of array and the parliamentarian militia commissioners to cease recruitment in an effort to prevent bloodshed (or to conclude a truce once fighting had begun). It should perhaps be emphasised that both groups were usually native to the county in which they were expected to recruit, and would probably be well acquainted with one another. The second group involved more extensive and ambitious plans to exclude the war completely from particular areas, in which the local community not only refused to fight each other, but sought to raise a local force to prevent others from entering the area. Into this category came the agreements in Lincolnshire, Staffordshire, Cheshire and other counties in the summer and autumn of 1642, and the famous Cheshire 'Treaty of Bunbury' in December 1642. The situation was summarised by Derek Hirst in his *Authority and Conflict, 1603-1658*:

1 Everywhere, men sought an escape in neutralism. The ruin of
Germany during the Thirty Years War, and the scattered agrarian
unrest that had broken out all over the country in 1640-42 as
political controls began to fracture, only reinforced the natural
5 human preference for peace. Even those whose loyalties were clear,
such as the parliamentarian Fairfaxes in Yorkshire, could recognise
how much they had to lose and strove to neutralise their own areas
- Sir John Hotham's fear lest 'the necessitous people ... set up for
themselves to the utter ruin of the nobility and gentry' was widely
10 shared. In county after county gentlemen shunned both the militia
ordinance and the commission of array.

The significance of these efforts to establish neutrality is threefold. In the
first place they emphasise how undivided and uncommitted in many
ways the country was. Far from rallying to either call and attacking their
neighbours in pursuit of the cause to which they were dedicated, most of
the gentry class, at least, seem to have reacted with uncertainty,
confusion and fear. Secondly, they demonstrate the powerful fear of
disorder which motivated many gentry efforts to keep the war from their
doors. While this operated in general terms to the benefit of the royalists,
it could equally persuade the county community to accept the presence
of either army if they could guarantee that military presence would
maintain order and control. Thirdly, they enhance the importance of the
individuals and minorities, like Cromwell in the eastern counties and the
Catholic gentry of Lancashire, who were committed to a cause and clear
about their intentions. The 'civil war in every county' described by Lucy
Hutchinson was in fact a battle between committed minorities, and the
prize was the allegiance, or at least acceptance of the result, by the
uncommitted majority.

Neutralism, was not a permanent option. It characterised the reaction
of many individuals to a situation which had got out of control, but once
war had started the demands of the committed parties, for support,
supplies and strategic advantage, would render their position untenable.
Neutrals would, in fact, be plundered by both sides. Hence the efforts at
local treaties, which would afford some protection, and the attempts to
organise local defence forces. In the end, as Hirst points out, they were
doomed to failure, but they have a significance which goes beyond the
simple human desire to avoid the danger and upheaval of war. What
these neutralist treaties also reveal, is the strength and importance of
local and county communities, and the loyalties to them which have
been labelled as 'localism'.

d) The Nature of Localism

Recent studies of county government and society in seventeenth-
century England have provided clear evidence of what has been termed

a localist perspective, emphasising the importance of the county community as an influence on outlook and behaviour. The treaties and agreements of the Civil War neutrals were not the work of individuals operating as independent units, but of community groups united by a shared perception of the locality and its needs. As Anthony Fletcher pointed out in studying *The Outbreak of the Civil War*, localism and neutralism were not exactly the same thing, although their effects could at times be similar. In many ways, seventeenth-century gentlemen belonged to their county first, and to their country second - indeed the word 'country' was more normally used at the time to describe a county or region than England as a whole. Although most gentlemen would spend a period of their youth at a university (Oxford and Cambridge were the only universities in England) and/or one of the Inns of Court in London, these were short interruptions of a life more normally spent in the management of an estate and the administration of local justice. Henry Oxinden, a Kentish gentleman, visited London once in his lifetime, while Mary Hyde, the mother of the future Lord Clarendon, never once left her native county of Wiltshire. For most of the gentry families, their county community, united by ties of blood, marriage and interest, and divided by local rivalries and issues more than national concerns, was the primary political unit. In the words of Alan Everitt, 'In some respects the England of 1640 resembled a union of partially independent states, rather as Canada today is a union of self-governing provinces, or America of federated states: and that union, as we all know, is not always a very simple or easy relationship'.

This did not mean that the members of these county communities had no views about the national issues of king, Church and parliament, nor that localism was equally powerful in all places and for all individuals. While counties such as Yorkshire, Cornwall and even Kent (for all its proximity to London) had strong and fairly self-contained communities, others like Warwickshire were more open and diffuse. Nevertheless, localism was a significant factor in much of the country, and its significance lies in its capacity to complicate the division of loyalties that occurred in 1642. A local perspective could influence decisions in a number of ways. In the first place, concern for the well-being of the local area could influence the willingness of individuals to participate fully in the struggle. For example, Sir George Booth of Cheshire was a committed supporter of parliament, who sent his tenants to defend the parliamentarian stronghold of Manchester - yet he also tried to negotiate an agreement with his royalist neighbour, Thomas Legh, to prevent the raising of any troops in Cheshire itself. In Kent Alan Everitt found that the majority of the gentry, moderate royalists and parliamentarians alike, were reluctant to participate in the struggle, which was essentially fought out by opposing minorities, many of whom had connections outside the county. Secondly, it could affect the choice of whom to support. In Staffordshire the neutrality pact was eventually abandoned in favour of the royalists, not because there were no parliamentarian sympathisers, but because the royalists were better-placed to assist in preventing lower-class disorders and preserve the peace of the county. Thirdly, localism could influence the taking of sides through the existence of local rivalries, particularly among those who were torn between conflicting beliefs and for whom the choice was therefore difficult. One clear example of this lies in the behaviour of Sir John Hotham, whose initial support of parliament was encouraged by dislike of the Wentworth influence in Yorkshire, and whose attempt to join the royalists in 1643 was equally forwarded by rivalry with the Fairfaxes. This point is reinforced by John Morrill, who showed in his *Revolt of the Provinces* that 'pre-existent power groupings within each county' had a good deal of influence on the taking of sides.

1 The overall effect of localism, therefore, is to complicate the task of deciding and describing how England divided in 1642; and this makes especially dangerous any attempt to draw upon this material to explain either the causes or the significance of the outbreak of
5 war. We cannot simply catalogue the actions that men took in choosing sides, or not, and make inferences from this about the extent and strength of support that each side enjoyed, let alone draw conclusions as to why. As Anthony Fletcher explained 'It is hard to believe ... that many well-informed men were pure neutrals
10 at heart. The leading men in the shires, and to some extent the same goes for mayors and aldermen, had been too much involved in the political debate to avoid adopting their own standpoints. Few surely saw a precisely equal amount of right on both sides. Yet at the same time everyone who was politically aware faced the
15 dilemma that by being true to their deepest feelings they might increase polarisation and destroy local peace. Thus commitment and activism were not the same things' - some men were committed but reluctant to take action, others active, but for motives other than a straightforward commitment; and some,
20 perhaps a majority, simply tried to balance their conflicting loyalties they best way they could.

e) The Loyalties of the People

Thus far, consideration has been given to the reactions of the social and political leaders - the gentry and the borough corporations - but any conclusions about the nature of divisions in England must also address the role and opinions of the common people of the time. It is difficult to assess the strength and nature of popular feeling in these circumstances, because the views of the ordinary citizen or peasant farmer were so rarely recorded. David Underdown and Derek Hirst have both shown that awareness of political issues extended well down the social scale. According to Underdown in his *Revel, Riot and Rebellion*, 'There is, in fact, plentiful evidence that in the early seventeenth century ordinary Englishmen had opinions on national issues that reflected their underlying concern for law, custom and 'good rule''. He argues that the nature of these concerns and their tendency to see the issues in local terms differs little from the attitudes displayed by the ruling elites. One source of evidence about popular attitudes can be found in the Quarter Sessions records, where prosecutions for seditious or insulting words can be commonly found. The records for Exeter in October-November 1642, for example, reveal a threat to poison the Prince of Wales who was resident nearby, a threat to open the town gates to the king's forces, and the singing of lewd songs about the king, the queen and the Earl of Manchester. Most of these incidents seem to have occurred in the various ale-houses of the city, but they probably serve to reveal genuine feeling even if there was little likelihood of the threats being carried out.

In so far as it is possible to interpret such scanty evidence, it would appear that ordinary citizens were indeed aware of the issues involved in the civil war, although not necessarily able to make free decisions about how to respond to them. According to contemporary commentators many tenants were expected or forced to follow the leadership of their lords; while independent craftsmen seem to have followed the cause of parliament. In neither case is it possible to generalise too freely. In boroughs such as Hull and Gloucester the decision about whom to support was made by the governor (if there was one) and corporation - but once made it was apparently widely accepted. Certainly the ordinary citizens of these towns played an active part in resisting royalist attacks. This may have arisen from respect for the town's governing body, from habits of accepting their authority, from genuine commitment, or from a mixture of all three. Equally likely, the requirements of survival may have dictated that the town should pull together in defence of home and property. The fate of towns which were taken by storm, or surrendered after a siege was not such as to encourage defenders to give up easily; plunder and looting was considered the soldiers' due. When Beverley surrendered without resistance to the royalist army as it approached Hull, the town was sacked and partly burned. The lesson would not have been lost on the citizens of Hull. Indeed the most reasonable conclusion about the views of ordinary citizens is that they reacted in exactly the same ways as others - some volunteered on principle, some sympathised with king and some with parliament, most were concerned with local needs and consequences, and ultimately, they sought to survive and protect what they had.

This evidence also suggests that, however the decisions of 1642-3 were taken, they were difficult to reverse. A town that surrendered would be liable to damage and destruction, no less than one which was taken by force. The experience of individuals who sought to change sides was not encouraging, as Hotham discovered. The Earls of Bedford, Holland and Clare, who left parliament in protest at the Scottish alliance of 1643, found themselves less than welcome at the Court of a king who sought victory rather than peace. When armies were defeated, it was common practice for both sides to recruit the rank and file into their own forces, but this was more difficult for the higher ranks. For the most part, the division of the country became more effective as both sides established administrative and military committees in the areas under their control. By mid-1643 the division of the nation had become a fact with which those who were thus divided had to live as best they could.

3 Assessment - A Nation Divided?

The argument above began with an account of the processes, issues and motivations which divided the nation between king and parliament, but the evidence provided thereafter raises serious doubts about how far this concept of clearcut division can be accepted as valid. In the autumn and winter of 1642-3 there is evidence of widespread neutralism and a reluctance to participate; in many areas the gentry joined ranks to protect their county community, whose needs and interests were at least as important as those of the two protagonists, the king and the parliament. Their efforts were doomed to failure, but the initial division of the country into royalist and parliamentarian areas had to be conducted through these county communities and with their agreement. This was to complicate the process and ultimately to allow committed minorities to seize the initiative and direct the decisions of the more uncertain majority. In these circumstances, individual, geographical, and sometimes random, factors could have considerable influence upon the outcome, and their effects could be difficult to reverse.

In the end, war did occur, and was sustained for several years. What Derek Hirst called 'fortress Staffordshire' and the other counties did fall to one side or another. Individuals chose to raise regiments for their cause, and there is evidence that hundreds, if not thousands, of men freely volunteered to fight. For a minority, an intensely committed minority, there were simple choices. On both sides there were those who knew where their priorities lay, and who acted quickly and decisively in pursuit of those priorities. On the royalist side, they were mainly fighting in defence of the king and the existing structure of society, in fear of the aspirations and ambitions of the lower orders, and sometimes through affection and respect for the Anglican Church. On the parliamentarian side there was loyalty to the parliament and the rule of law that it represented, fear of a royal tyranny that would deprive the individual of his rights and privileges, and above all, religious commitment - to Protestantism in its more radical forms, or at least to the defeat of popery. Among those for whom these choices were stark, there was a clear division. For the majority, however, there were divided loyalties - to king and to parliament, to the rule of law and the existing hierarchy, to the Protestant religion and the traditions of the Church, and above all, to the nation and the local community. Faced with a confusion of loyalties they tried to avoid a choice, and when forced to make it, did their best to live with the results. From 1642 to 1646 England was a nation divided, but not into two clear and coherent camps. In many ways the nation did not so much divide as fragment, with the fragments held together in two camps by war and necessity.

Making notes on 'A Nation Divided?'

The structure of the chapter is fairly straightforward, and for the purposes of note-making it can be taken one section at a time. The first section provides a chronological account of the process of division, and notes made in reasonable detail will provide an account of the first year of the war. Thereafter the approach is analytical, with each section focussing on a particular issue. These are not exhaustive accounts, but analytical points followed by examples and illustrations, and your notes should reflect this. Using the headings suggested below, the main points of argument can be used as sub-headings, followed in each case by some examples. The sources illustrate points made in the text, and where you take examples from a contemporary source, you should include the name of the source or author in your notes. Main headings could be:

1. How England divided
2. Motivating Factors   - Class
                          - Religion
3. Complicating Factors   - strategic location
                          - individual interests
                          - conflicting loyalties
                          - neutralism
                          - localism
4. Popular Feeling

Overall, your notes should allow you to explain how the country gradually took sides in the first year of war, what factors motivated individuals in making their choices, the reluctance with which many made such choices, and the problems involved in drawing any general conclusions or inferences about the causes of the war.

Answering essay questions on 'A Nation Divided?'

It is unlikely that you will be faced with essay questions based solely on the material contained in this chapter. The main value of this material is that it allows you to consider the motivation behind the taking up of

King		Parliament
Geographical loyalties		
West, South-west and Wales	Yorkshire / Midlands split and divided	London and South-east

Class loyalties

Aristocracy — →

Gentry — →

Middling sort (yeomen and craftsmen)

Tenantry (rural)

? Others ? ?

Pull Factors	**Pull Factors**
Social hierarchy	Social ambitions
Catholic / Anglican	Puritanism
Rural attitudes and structure	Urban attitudes and structure
Court influence	London influence

Cross-currents and complexities

Geographical proximity of main armies and strategic centres

Localism and Neutralism

Interaction of different and competing 'pull' factors

Individual / personal considerations and rivalries

Summary - A Nation Divided, 1642-3

arms, and therefore qualify the general conclusions about the causes of civil war that you have so far established. When considering *causation,* we tend to establish general patterns of behaviour or events: e.g. numerous examples of religious quarrels lead us to define religion as a *cause,* or *causal factor* of the event of civil war. The value of considering *motivation* is that it allows us to examine the variations that existed within the general patterns. For example, by asking the question "Why did men take up arms?" rather than "Why did war break out?", we have been led to the conclusion that religious issues were an important consideration for some, often key individuals in particular areas, but that others were motivated by more complex and often more mundane concerns. This does not invalidate the claim that religion was a cause of the war, but it does produce the more sophisticated conclusion that religious issues created a determined minority who were able to influence the actions of others, sometimes despite their own personal, social or local interests. We can also consider the depth and quality of support offered to one side or the other where these different interests clashed or coincided. Having established a number of causal factors in the outbreak of war at the end of Chapter 3, if we now try to consider how these factors motivated men to take up arms, we are able to explore their effects and importance more deeply and to produce a better explanation of why war occurred.

1. In the light of the information that you have gained from Chapter 4, reconsider your responses to the six essay questions listed at the end of Chapter 3. Working with a partner or in a group, discuss what changes or additions you would make.
2. Choose one essay question, and use the understanding that you have gained of both general causes and individual motives to plan and write a response.

Source-based questions on 'A Nation Divided?'

There is considerable variation in the nature and importance of the source-based questions used by the different examination boards, and you should try to collect and practise answering examples from past papers which are specific to the examination that you will take. However, the skills that are being tested do fall into two broad categories. The first relates to the ability to understand sources - testing comprehension, understanding of language, inference and deduction, and the ability to cross-reference and use sources together. The second builds on these essential skills by asking you to interpret and assess the significance of sources in a wider context, considering how far a source is reliable, typical or representative, and how far particular sources can be used as a basis for wider conclusions and generalisations. Because these are more complex skills, reliant on both personal judgements and wider knowledge, they usually carry more marks. The exercise below is more extensive and wide-ranging than a simple examination question, but seeks to take you through this hierarchy of skills, to demonstrate how they can be built up.

Taking Sides - an exercise in the evaluation and use of sources.
Re-read the sources drawn from accounts by Clarendon, Baxter, Lucy Hutchinson and Thomas May which are presented between pages 65 and 70.
a) Summarise the main points in Clarendon's description of the social and geographical division of the country on page 65. (Comprehension - 2 marks)
b) What does he mean by 'inferior people', 'natural malignity' and 'factious lecturers'? (Comprehension/interpretation - 3 marks)
c) What does he suggest were the main issues and motives that influenced this division? (Inference/generalisation - 4 marks)
d) In what ways does Baxter support Clarendon's views regarding i) patterns of allegiance, and ii) motivations? (Comprehension/cross-referencing - 3 marks)
e) In what ways do Baxter's views differ from those of Clarendon? (Interpretation/comparison - 5 marks)
f) What other factors are shown by Lucy Hutchinson and Thomas May to have affected how and why people took sides? (Comprehension/cross-referencing - 3 marks)
g) While not entirely differing in their interpretations, Clarendon emphasises the importance of social class while Baxter emphasises the importance of religion as motives in taking sides. In the light of all the sources and your wider knowledge, explain which interpretation you find most convincing. (Reliability/cross-referencing/ interpretation in context/evaluation - 12 marks)
h) Using all the sources and your own wider knowledge of the issues, produce an explanation of how and why people took sides that reconciles the different interpretations. (The question requires the application of all the skills practised above to produce an overall explanation which uses, but goes beyond, the sources provided - 18 marks)

CHAPTER 5

The Victory of Parliament, 1643-6

By the summer of 1643 the war appeared to be going the way of the king. After Prince Rupert's capture of Bristol (see page 64) the royalists were able to consolidate their hold on the west and link up the south-western counties with the royalist heartland of South Wales and the neighbouring districts in England. In August, Maurice captured Dorchester, gaining control of Dorset, and followed this up in September by taking Exeter. Only in Gloucester and Plymouth did sizeable parliamentarian garrisons hold out, and Gloucester at least seemed vulnerable to siege. In the north the royalists held most of the north-eastern counties and Newcastle's victory over the Fairfaxes at Adwalton Moor in June had secured control of Yorkshire. Only Hull, where the arrest of Hotham had retained the town for parliament and allowed the Fairfaxes to take refuge, still held out. There appeared to be little to prevent the king from carrying out his strategy of linking up his northern and western armies with his own at Oxford, and moving on towards London. With a respect for the London trained bands learned the previous year at Turnham Green, he intended to blockade the city and look to a rising of the citizens to bring about its fall. Nor was this an unlikely outcome, given the distress caused by parliamentary taxes and the increased hardship that such a blockade would create. Yet the march on London never came, and three years later, his options and resources exhausted, the king was forced to surrender. That he chose to surrender to the Scots rather than to parliament is evidence of his reluctance to admit defeat; but the overwhelming military superiority of parliament gave him no choice.

How, then, are we to explain such a remarkable change in the fortunes of the two protagonists? The answer lies in a combination of factors. For a variety of reasons, the king was unable to capitalise upon his early advantages. Secondly, the position of parliament was not as disastrous as it appeared, and included certain long-term advantages if survival could be secured for long enough to capitalise on them. That this occurred owed much to the tactical genius of John Pym. Thirdly, the needs and demands of war brought harder and more radical leaders to the fore in both camps, and this ultimately led to a military revolution in which parliament finally concentrated its considerable resources into a single, mobile and highly effective fighting force. In the end, it was the New Model Army which brought about a military victory for parliament. Ironically, its creation, its successes and its ideals made the task of establishing a political settlement thereafter, far more difficult.

1 The Failure of the Royalists

The king's position as monarch gave him a number of advantages in the early months of the war. He was able to call upon the loyalty of many of the gentry, and thus to acquire both money and skilled horsemen for his cavalry. The Earl of Worcester, for example, donated in the region of £300,000 before the war was over. According to Derek Hirst, the vast majority of the professional officer corps, many of whom were serving abroad in 1642, returned to serve the king. He was also able to call upon the support of foreign rulers, particularly his relatives in the United Provinces who had experience of war and abundant supplies of cavalry horses. Unlike parliament, he had a unified command and a clear strategy. For all of these reasons, he was able to organise and mobilise effective forces far more quickly than his opponents; the results were shown in the Edgehill campaign and in his early successes in 1643.

Historians have argued that these royalist advantages were dissipated by a failure of leadership, in which a hesitant king failed to develop an effective administration or to control his commanders adequately, so that the royalist war effort became fragmented. In some cases his more ruthlessly military commanders alienated local populations by allowing indiscriminate plunder, which contrasted with the discipline and restraint of the parliamentary troops. Eventually, the argument goes, neutrals and local resistance groups were driven to the side of parliament. As with many simple explanations, the argument contains valid elements and partial truths, but is by no means the whole story.

In many ways the royalist war effort followed the same pattern as that of parliament. In both cases recruiting by commissioners was resisted, and both sides relied initially on volunteers who raised individual regiments and troops from among their friends, neighbours and tenants. Later, both sides began, with some trepidation, forcibly to conscript for their armies. Where parliament placed county administration in the hands of the Lords Lieutenant, the king appointed six Lieutenant-Generals to administer the counties under royalist control. Co-ordination was provided by a Council of War at Oxford, similar to parliament's Committee of Safety. In both cases those appointed were chosen for their social and political status rather than their military or administrative expertise. In the light of experience, both sides became more efficient and more ruthless in their methods. By mid-1643 Charles had replaced early commanders such as the Marquess of Hertford with military leaders such as his nephews, Rupert and Maurice, and had begun to levy local rates in co-operation with civilian county committees similar to those of parliament. It is undoubtedly the case that these rates caused friction and were often in arrears. It is also true that they were sometimes forcibly collected, in kind, and that some commanders, such as Goring in Somerset, allowed local communities to be plundered regardless of their loyalties. Yet these problems were less a result of faults in the system than of the sheer weight and quantity of demands for supplies once the war passed its initial stages.

More accurate is the charge that Charles failed to control the conflicting aims and ambitions of his commanders and advisers. At certain times royalist strategy lacked direction, and in 1643 the failure of the northern and western armies to link up with Charles at Oxford destroyed what was probably the king's best chance of outright victory. Although there were rivalries involved, notably between Prince Rupert and Digby, the delay in the royalist advance also arose from military considerations. In Yorkshire, the Earl of Newcastle was reluctant to advance south while leaving a parliamentary force in Hull to harry his rear; he may also have been concerned by a threat of intervention from Scotland. The western forces were similarly delayed by the sieges of Gloucester and Plymouth. Newcastle has been criticised for his decision, particularly as Hull's position and parliament's naval strength made the town difficult to besiege successfully, but both Hull and Gloucester did constitute a threat to vital supply lines. As it was, the king himself began the siege of Gloucester in August and the town was relieved by Essex in September. When the king tried to prevent Essex's return to London, he was defeated at the battle of Newbury on 20 September. Thereafter, a successful attack on London was unlikely, and he withdrew to Oxford. Three weeks later Fairfax broke the siege of Hull, and a few days later the success of Cromwell and Fairfax at Winceby in Lincolnshire secured control of the Humber estuary and its southern bank. Newcastle therefore abandoned the siege on the same day, 11 October.

While there is no doubt of the importance of these failures, and that royalist rivalries were partially responsible for the priority given to the regional campaigns, it cannot be said that failures of leadership on the part of the king were entirely, or perhaps even mainly responsible. More serious was the division within the royalist ranks over the ultimate objectives of the fighting. While Edward Hyde and the moderates sought to find a negotiated settlement, and to win over moderate opinion, it was increasingly clear that the king aimed at military victory and listened most closely to the advice of the queen, militarists like Rupert, and the extremist Lord Digby. In 1643 when the moderate Lord Falkland was killed in the fighting, he was replaced by Digby as Secretary of State. Thus, while the king delayed the levying of a county rate until 1643, and sought to maintain legal forms in order to placate local opinion, he increasingly undid the effect of this by the influence given to militarist advisers. The clearest example of these errors came in the autumn of 1643 when he retaliated against parliament's Scottish alliance by agreeing a Cessation (truce) with the Catholic rebels in Ireland. His purpose was to free the experienced English troops engaged in Ireland in order to use them himself, but given contemporary attitudes towards the Irish, he granted his opponents an enormous propaganda victory. Rumours of Irish Catholic troops and Irish atrocities in England abounded. More immediately, the carefully laid plans constructed by Hyde to capitalise on anti-Scottish sentiment, both within and outside parliament, were swept aside by the spate of anti-Catholic feeling and the apparent confirmation that the king was conspiring with Irish Catholic rebels.

It is true, therefore, that royalist administration was imperfect, that royalist strategy was uncertain and that the royalist leadership was, at times, divided. Nevertheless, these failings were mirrored by their opponents, whose weaknesses, uncertainties and divisions were as great or greater than those in the royalist camp. What made the royalist weaknesses so much more damaging were two factors - first, that they had fewer resources and long-term advantages to squander, and secondly, that the effect of parliament's weaknesses was minimised by the work and achievements of John Pym. The fact was that the counties under royalist control, the north, south-west and west midlands, were poorer than the parliamentarian south-east, and the midland counties were also the scene of constant fierce fighting. Parliamentary garrisons such as that at Gloucester were not only strategically important, but were also able to harry and harass the countryside upon which the royal armies depended. With parliament in control of the navy and of most of the major ports, the king was never able to make full use of his foreign allies. The cavaliers who left their estates in order to serve the king were increasingly less able to bear the burdens of financing him. In short, the king's strengths and advantages were most valuable for a short war and a rapid strike - and once that had failed, the advantage would slowly move towards parliament.

In these circumstances, the royalist failings took on a more crucial importance. The king did build up a more effective military and administrative system, but the delay was costly. Individual errors of strategy in 1643 were damaging because they wasted diminishing opportunities. However, this did not mean that a parliamentarian victory became inevitable thereafter. What was so crucial about the royalists' failures in 1642-3 was that they allowed the parliament to survive its darkest hours, and to begin to utilise the resources at its disposal. In the long run these were greatly superior to their own.

2 The Assets of Parliament

The strengths and weaknesses of the parliamentary cause were almost exactly opposite to those of the king. Where the king had a unified command and administration, parliament had to rely on a series of overlapping committees, whose ability to initiate new and more efficient systems was limited. Reliance upon county and local militias made military planning even more difficult, and only in the moments of greatest danger did the county committees overcome local concerns and effectively pool their resources. They did, however, maintain links with local support, which proved to be of benefit in the long run in preventing some of the military abuses that created anti-royalist feeling in counties such as Somerset. Control of the navy was of great strategic importance, especially in the long term, and the resources of the parliamentary heartland in the south-east were substantial once the means of drawing on them was established.

The political divisions that beset the royalists were magnified within a parliament of nearly two hundred, many of whom were, and remained, backbench MPs with limited appreciation of what war would involve. While many were capable of contributing, time and experience were required. The more influential members fell into three main groups. The 'peace party' was led by a number of Lords and by Denzil Holles in the Commons and had strictly limited and defensive war aims. The 'war party', led by Sir Henry Vane, Sir Arthur Haselrig and the republican Henry Marten, openly sought the total defeat of the king as a prelude to severely reducing his powers. Linking and organising these forces were a middle group led by Pym, with the help of Oliver St. John, John Hampden and Oliver Cromwell, who sought a negotiated settlement which would include control over the armed forces and the king's advisers. The purpose, and achievement, of this group was to hold together this fragile coalition while developing the measures needed to fight a war. While the king needed to strike and act quickly, the parliamentary cause would require time to organise, develop, and tap its considerable resources.

That this time was found and used constructively was due, in no small measure to the leadership of John Pym. In the first year of the war his greatest achievements lay in two areas - his ability to utilise the dangers and disasters of the military situation to persuade conservative MPs to adopt radical measures, and his ability to hold together the peace and war parties despite their conflicting aims. Thus he used the failure at Edgehill and Rupert's assault on Brentford to persuade MPs to establish compulsory weekly assessments (taxes) in London, which were later extended to other areas. By persuading parliament to thus assume powers of taxation, extended by the introduction of an excise tax after the breakdown of peace negotiations at Oxford in the spring of 1643, he laid the basis of a reasonably effective financial structure. In December 1642 he was able to reduce localist obstruction, at least a little, by establishing the Midland and Eastern Associations to co-ordinate county administration and military effort. Nevertheless, the benefits of these measures would take time to be felt, and in the meantime, royalist success threatened to make them irrelevent. Royalist delays, the determined resistance of Hull and Gloucester, and the unexpected success of the Eastern Association armies, along with Essex's victory at Newbury, saved parliament that summer. Pym utilised the time given, as well as the fears aroused, to introduce a new strategy - an alliance with the battle-hardened army of the Scottish Covenanters.

While such a strategy might well seem obvious, to contemporaries it was both dangerous and unwelcome. The Scots rebels had enabled the opposition in the Long Parliament to challenge Charles, but they were far from popular in England. To long-standing anti-Scottish sentiment could be added a dislike of the rigid brand of Presbyterianism adopted by the Scottish Kirk, even among those of puritan sympathies, and there was no doubt that a religious settlement of this kind would be the price of Scottish support. To many of the moderates, this had another disadvantage - it would make a negotiated settlement with the king even harder to achieve, since his genuine devotion to the Anglican Church would not allow him to accept a Presbyterian settlement. The specific association of the parliamentary cause with Presbyterian reform in the Church threatened their hopes of peace, and tied them to an obligation for which many moderates had little liking. By bringing in another party who might well claim a place at any negotiating table, Pym was complicating the process and reducing its chances of success. By bringing the Scots into the armed conflict, he was also widening the scope of war and changing its character. To those who sought a peace based on minimising differences with the royalists and reaching a rapid compromise, the Scottish Covenanters and their religious crusade appeared to be disastrous allies.

With considerable skill Pym met these difficulties and pushed his strategy through. He avoided a total commitment to Scottish Presbyterianism by agreeing to call an Assembly of Ministers to devise a scheme of reform. The details of this scheme were to be settled 'as may be agreeable to God's Holy Word' - a form of words which both pre-empted criticism and invited months, if not years, of debate before any final decisions could be made. He blocked a new peace initiative on the basis that, given parliament's weakness at this time, the only negotiation that the king would accept would be their surrender. Shortly afterwards, however, he secured the expulsion of the republican Henry Marten from the Commons, in a move that reassured many of the peace party, as well as removing the most aggressive leader of the war party. Finally, Charles himself sealed Pym's success in holding together the parliamentary coalition by concluding his Irish Cessation, and raising once more the spectre of popery.

Therefore, when Pym died in December 1643 he had steered the parliamentary cause through its most difficult period and had laid the base for future development. The military situation was one of stalemate, but parliament had acquired a powerful ally whose value would be shown in the following year. The system of administration was adequate, and the financial reforms of the spring were at last beginning to bear fruit. With the rich south-eastern counties securely under control, the support of the navy and the Scottish alliance, those who took over Pym's role had at least the basic material for success.

3 The Achievement of Victory

That success was by no means assured or automatic. Although Pym had persuaded parliament to accept the Scottish alliance, stresses and tensions remained, to which the Scots themselves contributed by their continuing efforts to obtain the establishment of a Presbyterian Church in England. In the spring of 1644 St. John and Vane, supported by Lord Saye and Sele in the Lords, succeeded in reducing the power of the peace party by re-organising the parliamentary administration. The old Committee of Safety was replaced by a Committee of Both Kingdoms upon which the war and middle parties were more strongly represented. Unfortunately this offended the military commander, the Earl of Essex, especially when the committee diverted some resources to the armies of Manchester and Waller in the south-east. Although Manchester's Eastern Association army was already proving the most effective of the parliamentary forces, its value was undermined by a localist outlook which limited its sphere of operations. While the Scots army remained in the north, besieging the city of Newcastle, the parliamentary forces in the south squabbled, failed to co-ordinate, and suffered a serious defeat at Cropredy Bridge in Oxfordshire in June 1644. Beset by political and military divisions at the centre, the parliamentary cause was rescued by one of its more peripheral associations - the Yorkshire armies led by Fairfax.

The retreat to Hull in 1643 and the successful resistance against Newcastle's siege had given the Yorkshire army the opportunity to regroup. In January 1644 Sir Thomas Fairfax had destroyed the biggest contingent of Charles's Irish forces (released by the Cessation) at Nantwich in Cheshire, before turning east to link up with the Scots. By April Fairfax had succeeded, with the help of a Scottish contingent, in forcing Newcastle's army back into York, where they were now besieged. Realising the strategic importance of his northern army, and of York itself, Charles sent Prince Rupert to relieve the city - a mission in which he was successful. Unfortunately, however, Rupert then chose to meet the parliamentary forces in open battle, despite the fact that Manchester and Cromwell had now brought the Eastern Association army to reinforce Fairfax and the Scots, and bring the parliamentary total to 28,000 men. On 2 July the armies clashed at Marston Moor, and after a fierce struggle, the royalist army was broken. York surrendered two weeks later.

The battle of Marston Moor was of enormous significance in the war, yet its military importance was less than might have been expected. Certainly it secured the north for parliament, and reduced royalist control to its western heartlands, but there were some strategic advantages in a geographically compact military base. Moreover, beset by internal differences, the parliamentary forces failed to follow up their military advantage. It is even possible that the success of his rivals actually goaded the discontented Essex into his most disastrous error - a march west in search of an equally spectacular victory against the king's western armies. He succeeded in relieving the besieged Lyme, in Dorset, but then allowed himself to be trapped in the south-western peninsula, eventually abandoning his entire army in Cornwall. Having received the surrender of both the men and their supplies and weaponry, the victorious royalists turned east, to be met by a reluctant and internally divided Eastern Association at Newbury in Berkshire, in a battle which ended as a losing draw for the parliamentarians. Militarily the situation had ended once more in stalemate, and the gains of Marston Moor had been dissipated.

Politically, however, the battle was to have far-reaching effects in bringing to the surface the underlying tensions and differences that divided the parliamentary movement. The political differences between the peace and war parties partly reflected, and were certainly complicated by, religious issues which the Scottish presence helped to intensify. Few conservative parliamentarians were committed to any form of Presbyterianism, least of all the Scottish model, but they were concerned about order and social discipline, and regarded a national Church based on authority and compulsion as essential in maintaining such controls. From the time of the collapse of censorship in 1641, they had been concerned at the spate of radical pamphlets and activities of religious separatists which had been permitted, and which had increased with the outbreak of war. Nowhere had these enthusiasts found a more sympathetic response than in the army of the Eastern Association, where both Cromwell and Manchester had sought to recruit men of religious zeal and commitment to the cause. Moreover, when such men distinguished themselves by their effort and dedication, they were promoted in the name of efficiency and military effectiveness. These policies had contributed a great deal to success of the Eastern Association, and particularly in the creation of a cavalry whose courage matched, and whose discipline outshone, the royalists. It was Cromwell's cavalry which tipped the balance at Marston Moor when, unlike Rupert's successful forces on the other wing of the battle, it had sufficient discipline to regroup and attack the royalist centre to destroy Newcastle's infantry. The problem for the more cautious parliamentarians was that militarily they needed such men while, politically, they feared them.

By raising the issue of the future organisation of the Church, the Scottish alliance had crystallised such fears. When separatist demands for a measure of religious toleration emerged within the Assembly of Divines itself, concern grew, complaints multiplied, and Manchester's Scottish major-general, Crawford, sought to reassert control within the Eastern Association army. His attempts to purge separatist officers and discipline soldiers for preaching in the place of ordained ministers had already led to bitter quarrels with Cromwell before Marston Moor, but the battle increased tensions in several ways. When Cromwell and others saw at first hand the rigid Presbyterianism of the Scots, they were confirmed in their determination to oppose it. When victory came through their efforts rather than those of the Scots, they were confirmed in their conviction that they had God's approval; and when conservatives, Scottish and English alike, saw the effectiveness of Cromwell's 'godly party' they determined to reduce their power and number.

It was in this context that a bitter power struggle broke out within the parliamentarian ranks, in which the competing and overlapping aims of three parties created a confusion of shifting factions and enmities. In parliament the middle group was already finding itself closer to the so-called war party. Within the army of the Eastern Association, open feuding occurred between the supporters of Cromwell and the Presbyterian officers, in which each side promoted men of their own persuasion and sought to purge their opponents. Manchester was unable to control the effects of this squabbling, and the military results were seen in the failure at Newbury. When the war party in the Commons attacked Essex, the peace group and the Presbyterians were able to counter-attack at the expense of Cromwell. Manchester himself seems to have become convinced of the futility of the struggle against the king, declaring that 'if we fight a hundred times and beat him ninety and nine times, he will be king still... But if he beat us but once, or the last time, we shall be hanged.' When the crisis came to a head, he aligned himself with the conservatives. In imminent danger of political defeat, Cromwell and his allies in parliament outflanked their opponents with the introduction of the Self-denying Ordinance in December 1644.

The Ordinance admitted fault on all sides, and proposed a separation of military and political functions which would create a new, central army led by military men. It would thus remove all members of parliament from within this army and allow it to function without political interference. It had the attraction of providing a military re-organisation which all parties could see the need for, and a solution to the political deadlock in which the parliamentarians were trapped. As members of the House of Lords, the old generals would lose their places, without personal humiliation. Since the main purpose of the war party was to win the war, this in itself would serve their aims. The Ordinance was quickly accepted by the Commons, but met with stiff opposition in the Lords whose members would be the greatest losers. While the Lords wrangled, however, proof of the need for a military victory came from the king at Oxford. Under pressure from the Scots new negotiations had been opened, with parliamentary and Scottish commissioners meeting the king at Uxbridge. Not only did Charles reiterate his old position, but the Scottish insistence on a Presbyterian Church opened new disputes (see Appendix). By January 1645 it was clear that a negotiated settlement was as far away as ever, and the Lords had little choice but to accept the Ordinance. Thereafter, attention turned to the appointment of its leading officers. The Lord General was Sir Thomas Fairfax, a man of moderate puritan convictions and good military reputation. His

Major-General of the Infantry was Philip Skippon, another moderate
who had led the London Trained Bands to victory at Turnham Green in
1642. No Lieutenant-General of the Horse could be agreed upon by the
Lords, and so at last Fairfax requested that he be served by Oliver
Cromwell on a temporary basis, until agreement could be reached.

The outcome could hardly have been better for the war party.
Cromwell continued to serve on a series of three month commissions
and was able to contribute his considerable abilities to the formation of a
new and highly effective fighting force. The New Model Army did not
spring into being immediately as a military miracle. It was based upon
existing regiments, many of its officers were gentlemen of social status,
and many of the rank and file were pressed men or professional soldiers
interested only in their pay. Nevertheless it had great advantages over its
predecessors. It was for the most part fairly well paid, it was well-drilled
and disciplined, and it was not attached to any regional location. One of
the main reasons for the speed with which the New Model was to mop
up the remaining royalist forces in 1645-6 was the rapidity with which it
could move, bringing its full force to bear upon an enemy whose forces
remained divided and fragmented. Perhaps most important of all, the
core of the New Model came from the old army of the Eastern
Association and carried over the principles of promotion by merit,
religious enthusiasm and godly discipline that had begun to make that
army such a formidable fighting unit. In the short term the military
advantages of this were significant; in the long term the political effects
would be even more so.

For the moment the military issue was paramount, and it is ironic that
the first major success of the New Model was to be provided in many
ways by the king. In the spring of 1645 Charles was torn between two
strategies. On the one hand he could relieve his port of Chester and try
to join up with his Scottish supporters under Montrose to re-open the
struggle for the north. On the other hand, it made good sense to attack
the New Model while it was in its formative stages. Opinion within the
royalist camp differed, with Rupert and Digby bitterly at odds.
Characteristically, Charles tried to do both, and by dividing his forces
left both armies outnumbered. Even so, Rupert would probably have
avoided the worst effects had not Digby pushed the king into insisting
that they attack a larger New Model which was occupying a strong
position outside the Leicestershire village of Naseby. The result, on 14
June 1645, was disaster. The parliamentary left flank was driven back by
Rupert's cavalry, which promptly left the field of battle, but once more
Cromwell's Eastern Association cavalry held firm and, having driven
their royalist counterparts from the field, regrouped and destroyed the
royalist infantry. The loss of his main army was bad enough for Charles,
but worse was to come. When the royalist baggage-train was captured,
the king's private correspondence came into parliamentarian hands.
When it was published it revealed the extent of his duplicity. In the

words of Derek Hirst:

1 The king's captured correspondence, published by parliament as
  The King's Cabinet Opened, revealed to the world his contempt for
  peace negotiations and his attempts to gain aid from all and
  sundry, including the Catholic Irish and the Pope; one leading
5 Welsh royalist, Sir Trevor Williams, promptly changed sides.
  Meanwhile Cromwell and others grew more confident that the
  hand of God was with them.

The battle of Naseby was a turning-point, but it was not the end of the
war. It destroyed the king's main field army, but there were other
royalist forces, besides the countless local garrisons and fortified houses.
Moreover, the king himself remained at large, and had no intention of

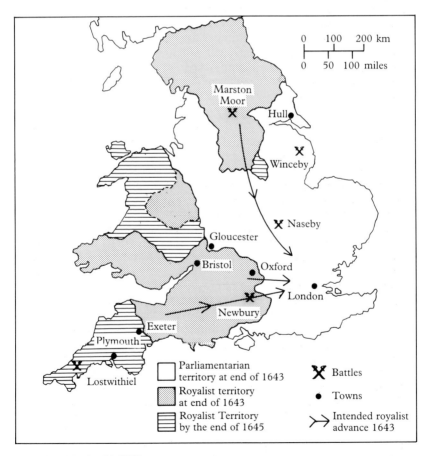

England in the Civil War

giving up. However, there can be no doubt that the balance had swung decisively in favour of parliament. The New Model had gained in confidence and experience, and was able to follow up its victory by setting off in pursuit of the other main royalist army, which was commanded by Goring in Somerset. There Fairfax found local support in a population whom Goring had mistreated and suppressed, and in July Goring was defeated at Langport. Two months later, on 10 September, Rupert surrendered the last remaining royalist stronghold in the south-west - the port of Bristol, in which the garrison was starving and the plague rife. It says much about the uncle whom he had faithfully served, that Charles never forgave this 'betrayal'.

Yet the collapse of the royalist cause in England was not only the result of the successes of the New Model, but came equally from the resurgence of an older enemy - the forces of neutralism which reappeared in royalist areas with a strength born of war-weariness and desperation. The burdens of war had been enormous - not only in providing men and arms, but in supporting both main armies and local garrisons - and these burdens had fallen on a population already suffering from depression, unemployment and the dislocation of trade. The problems are illustrated in a letter written to Viscount Fairfax (cousin of the parliamentarian general) from his agent at Alne, in Yorkshire, detailing the condition of his estates in May 1645:

> 1 I presently went to your tenants of your several manors to demand arrears. The answer of them all was ... that [with] the assessments paid to the armies, they were scarce able to pay anything. The tenants of Acaster Malbis ... had prepared a petition ... for relief,
> 5 having sustained above £2000 damage by the Scots... Skelton and Ampleforth, Gilling and Coulton lay so near Helmsley castle that during the time it was besieged, they were never without soldiers upon free billet ...who, besides their other provisions which they ate up, killed all their sheep.

By 1645 the whole country was impoverished and weary of war and for many the overriding concern was peace and survival. This growing demand for an end to the fighting was not directed towards helping one side rather than the other, although in specific areas neutralist groups did make alliances with the main protagonists when it suited their purpose. The aim of neutralism was peace, but in the circumstances of 1645, it worked to the benefit of parliament rather than the king.

4 The Resurgence of Neutralism, 1644-5

The first signs of the resurgence of neutralism came in the western counties held by the royalists, especially along the borders of Wales, and in South Wales itself. The defeats of 1644 had weakened the royalist grip

The Souldiers in their passage to York, turn unto reformers pull down Popish pictures, break down rayles, turn altars into Tables.

Both sides sought to exploit propaganda opportunities throughout the war, as the prints above show

in these areas, and the continuing existence of parliamentarian enclaves ensured heavy fighting and a heavy burden of rates. While claims that the royalist troops were less disciplined than those of parliament can be exaggerated, it was certainly true of some regiments, and the greater difficulties in keeping them regularly paid and supplied increased any tendency to indiscriminate looting.

For all of these reasons, it was the royalist cause which suffered more from the re-emergence of localism, and in particular the formation of Clubmen Associations. These were usually peasant associations, formed to protect property and supplies, which were often taken over and more fully organised by local gentry. They set out demands for a national peace and sought meanwhile to obtain an effective truce in their own areas. There was no standard format. In Somerset the initial impetus came from a group of royalist gentry in the winter of 1644-5, who sought to establish a local association that would work in conjunction with the king's forces. This was copied in Worcestershire, Herefordshire, Shropshire and Staffordshire where the gentry formed an association to impose local order and control the provisioning and maintenance of the royalist troops in the area. Again, this was not overtly anti-royalist, but sought to put local needs first and to regain control of the locality.

In January and March, 1645, however, there were popular risings in these counties, which demanded the removal of all troops from the area. The response of the royalist generals was to make concessions to the gentry associations, and to crush the peasant risings. They could not, however, retain control of the situation, particularly after the destruction of the main royalist army at Naseby in June 1645. When the New Model Army advanced into Somerset they found the Clubmen Associations of Wiltshire, Dorset and Somerset willing to co-operate in the effort to drive out the remaining royalists. This was not a matter of support for parliament, but a desire to regain control of the county, as their articles of Association illustrate:

1 The Desires and resolutions of the counties of Dorset and Wiltshire (Summer 1645)
   First: to maintain and defend the true reformed Protestant religion, and the inheritance of the crown.
5 Secondly: to join with and assist one another in the mutual defence of our liberties and properties, against all plunderers and against all other unlawful violence whatsoever ...

In this case the behaviour of Goring's royalist troops in plundering the area and the contrasting discipline of the New Model encouraged a tactical alliance between the Clubmen and the forces of parliament. Similarly, in the autumn of 1645 the Associations of South Wales were to declare for parliament, although a year later they were re-formed in an attempt to drive out the parliamentarian troops. The difference was that the latter retained the ability to respond, and the rising was crushed. The articles of the Sussex Clubmen of September 1645 were clearly directed against the parliamentary administration from which they had suffered, particularly in their complaints against unlicensed preachers and the 'want of Church government'. Again, however, the parliamentary cause suffered less because the administration had the power to deal with any disturbances.

The Clubmen Associations revealed the general unpopularity of the war, and raise doubts about the extent to which the population as a whole was ever committed to either cause. In practice, once the balance had tipped in favour of parliament, they did much to hasten the collapse of the royalist cause, but they were motivated less by a desire for parliamentary victory than by a wish to protect their own locality, or at most to see a speedy end to the war. As John Morrill put it,

> 1 There is overwhelming evidence that most of the Clubmen were neutrals ... This certainly did not preclude Associations from assisting either king or parliament in particular circumstances, but this need not imply a betrayal of their neutralism. A tactical
> 5 alliance with Fairfax, for example, helped the Devon and southern Somerset Clubmen to rid themselves of Goring, who represented a threat to provincial liberties far greater than that posed, in the short term, by the New Model. The Clubmen were not seeking to help parliament win the war. They were using parliamentary troops to
> 10 clear their own counties of the most potent immediate threat.

Whatever their aims, however, the Clubmen movements worked to the benefit of parliament in weakening the royalist grip on its last remaining heartland. In the winter of 1645-6 the king remained at Oxford, seeking some strategy that might save him from surrender. Montrose and his Scottish supporters had been destroyed in September 1645, attempting to obey the king's command to come southward to his aid. Early in 1646 Charles offered to make Catholicism the official religion of Ireland if the Irish Confederates (the Catholic rebels) would come to his aid. Such desperate strategies achieved little as the New Model continued to mop up remaining royalist garrisons and strongholds. Finally, accepting the inevitable yet too proud to submit to a parliament, Charles left Oxford in April 1646 and gave himself into the custody of the Scots. Held at Newcastle, he listened to their proposals for Presbyterianism and received the Propositions of his English parliament for a diluted Presbyterianism in the Church and parliamentary control of the militia. He accepted neither, and, infuriated by his lack of response, the Scots gladly handed him over to the safe-keeping of parliament and withdrew from England (with a payment of £400,000 for their trouble). As Robert Baillie, one of the Scottish commissioners in

London, predicted gloomily, 'that madman... will [take] down with
him all his posterity, and monarchy'.

5 Conclusion - The Victory of Parliament

Parliament's victory resulted from a combination of factors whose role
and importance in the final outcome needs to be carefully assessed. One
way of doing this to consider which factors were conditional, creating an
underlying probability of parliamentary victory, as opposed to those
contingent factors which turned the probability into fact and influenced
its shape and timing. These categories can also be used to assess the
relative importance of different factors, and to show what combination
of factors ultimately led to the victory of parliament.

It is clear that parliamentary control of the south-east and London
provided superior resources, and that possession of the navy and the
major ports of the kingdom enabled the parliament to stop the king from
redressing the balance with supplies from abroad. Thus one factor in
parliament's success was its underlying superiority of resources. Time
was required, however, to access these resources fully, and the initial
advantage lay with the king. Hence the royalist failures of 1642-3 were
also crucial. Determined resistance by pockets of parliamentary support
- in particular, the London trained bands after Edgehill and the ports of
Hull, Plymouth and Gloucester in 1643 - contributed to these, but the
rivalries and differences among the royalist commanders were equally, if
not more important. Newcastle's failure to march south in the summer
of 1643 prevented an attack on London when parliamentarian fortunes
were at their lowest ebb, and the continuing disputes between Prince
Rupert and Lord Digby meant that strategic decisions were often
influenced by personal considerations. Ultimately this failure of
leadership must rest with the king, who had an authority denied to the
parliamentary leaders. His hesitations and uncertainties, as well as the
lack of judgement in choosing his advisers that he had shown all his life,
contributed in no small measure to the royalist failure.

If royalist errors prevented an early royalist victory, they did not
ensure parliamentary success. Without effective leadership, parliament
would have been unable to use the breathing-space provided. Thus the
skill of John Pym in balancing the opposing parties within the
Commons, in persuading members to adopt new and unpopular
methods of administration, and to accept a Scottish alliance was
essential. As a result, the balance swung in favour of parliament, and it
can be argued that the factors outlined so far created the probability, or
likelihood, that the parliamentary forces would win the war, but this was
by no means certain. The failure of Essex in Cornwall showed how easily
mistakes could be made, and resources drained. The final condition
necessary for parliament's victory came with the military re-organisation
of 1644-5, the emergence of leaders who sought victory as the

pre-requisite of peace, and the establishment of the New Model Army. Thereafter, it is difficult to see that a royalist victory could have been possible.

If parliamentary victory was now inevitable at some time, it was by no means certain that it would be quick or complete. It was Charles's tactical error in fighting the battle of Naseby, and the re-emergence of neutralism, that brought royalist collapse within little more than a year. These contingent factors did much to speed up the process, but with resources already stretched and rivalries continuing, it is difficult to believe that the royalists were capable of matching the effectiveness of the New Model, or of reorganising themselves to become so. Had they been able to buy time it is perhaps possible that new divisions might have emerged in parliament, but the key factors in the ultimate outcome were already in place. By 1645 the combination of superior resources, superior leadership and superior military organisation had established the essential conditions for parliamentary victory.

***Making notes on** 'The Victory of Parliament'*

The introduction to this chapter picks out the main factors that contributed to parliament's victory, while the ensuing argument explains parliament's success more fully through a broadly chronological structure. It is therefore best to approach note-making by using the structure of the chapter and breaking its sections down into sub-sections such as those suggested below.

1. The failure of the Royalists
   (a) leadership
   (b) internal divisions
   (c) limited resources
2. Parliamentary Assets
   (a) military assets
   (b) financial resources
   (c) problems - accessing resources - internal divisions
   (d) leadership of Pym - organisation - maintaining unity - Scottish alliance
3. Parliamentary victory
   (a) Pym's successors
   (b) Marston Moor; victory in the North
   (c) political crisis and religious divisions
   (d) the Self-Denying Ordinance; the victory of the 'war' party
   (e) military reorganisation; the New Model Army
   (f) Naseby; the turning-point
4. The resurgence of Neutralism - the final phase and collapse of the Royalists

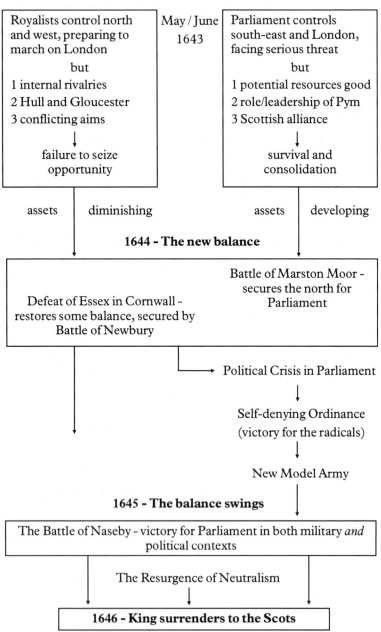

1643 – The two sides

	May / June 1643	
Royalists control north and west, preparing to march on London		Parliament controls south-east and London, facing serious threat
but		but
1 internal rivalries		1 potential resources good
2 Hull and Gloucester		2 role/leadership of Pym
3 conflicting aims		3 Scottish alliance
failure to seize opportunity		survival and consolidation

assets   diminishing   assets   developing

1644 – The new balance

Defeat of Essex in Cornwall - restores some balance, secured by Battle of Newbury	Battle of Marston Moor - secures the north for Parliament

Political Crisis in Parliament

Self-denying Ordinance (victory for the radicals)

New Model Army

1645 – The balance swings

The Battle of Naseby - victory for Parliament in both military *and* political contexts

The Resurgence of Neutralism

1646 – King surrenders to the Scots

Summary – The Victory of Parliament, 1643-6

These notes should provide i) a brief chronological outline of the course of the war between 1643 and 1646, and ii) an explanation of the main reasons for, and key stages in the parliamentary victory. It would also be useful to summarise separately the role of key individuals such as the king, Pym, and the military leaders on both sides.

Answering essay questions on 'The Victory of Parliament'

Like the outbreak of war in Chapter 3, the victory of parliament is usually treated as an event, to be explained by identifying and examining a number of causal factors. Essay questions on the issue can take a wide variety of forms, for example:-

1. Why was parliament, rather than the king, victorious in the first Civil War, 1642-6?
2. To what extent was parliament's victory in 1646 inevitable?
3. 'A story of weak leadership and lost opportunities.' Does this accurately describe the reasons for royalist defeat in the first Civil War, 1642-6?
4. How far was Pym the architect of parliamentary victory in the first Civil War?
5. 'It was the New Model Army that gave victory to parliament.' How far do you agree with this judgement?

Question 1 sets out the issue in a straightforward fashion, while the other four questions all focus on particular factors which must be explained, and then assessed against other contributory elements. Question 2 places stress on the underlying trend and balance of forces, while 3, 4 and 5 emphasise more specific elements which shaped and influenced the way in which those forces operated. In all cases, a good response demands that all of these factors be examined and their relative importance compared and assessed.

One way of doing this, as demonstrated in the concluding section of the chapter, is to identify some factors as *conditional* and others as *contingent*. Historians often discuss causes as being long-term, or underlying, by which they mean that certain factors have built up over a period to create an underlying situation that makes a particular outcome possible or likely. Other causes are seen as short-term and less deep-rooted, influencing the timing, detail or precise form of that outcome. A more exact way of defining such factors is offered by the terms conditional and contingent. Conditional factors are those which create underlying conditions in which a particular event or outcome is likely. These are often long-term (such as the growth of religious discontent before the outbreak of war) but not always. For example, one vital condition which made war possible in 1642, was the collapse of parliamentary unity in the second half of 1641, without which the king could not have raised a 'side' to fight for him. Contingent factors, on the other hand, are those which trigger an event at a particular time, or dictate the precise nature of the outcome. These do tend to be short-term, and are often related to individual actions or specific events. For example, a contingent event in the outbreak of war in 1642 was the Irish Rebellion, which created an immediate crisis and broke the stalemate of 1641.

1. Re-read the final section (Conclusion) of this chapter, and using that and your own notes and ideas, construct a list of factors that contributed to the victory of parliament. Label each factor as conditional (creating the conditions which made parliamentary victory likely) or contingent (influencing when and how it occurred).

2. Compare your ideas with those of others. To do this, you will have to explain exactly what part you think each factor played in the parliamentary victory. Do not be surprised if there is some variation, both in the way you have defined particular factors and the part that they played. This is particularly likely in relation to the role of individual leaders like the king or Pym, whose character and talents can be seen as conditional, but whose actions and errors had particular contingent effects.

3. Use these definitions to consider the relative importance of different factors. This largely involves weighing up the importance of the underlying balance of forces against the actions and decisions of the individuals and groups who used them. There are, however, some interesting elements to consider - for example, would parliament's underlying resources and assets have been important, had royalist mistakes and/or Pym's skill not given them time to be developed and realised?

4. In the light of these considerations and discussions, choose one of the essays listed to plan and write. Remember that the essay question will indicate the starting-point for your argument, but that you will need to consider all the factors that you have defined and to compare the role of any factor specified by the question against the influence of other factors in the whole combination.

***Source-based questions on** 'The Victory of Parliament'*

The purpose of the source-based questions set out below is to allow you to practise and develop the skills outlined in the study guide at the end of Chapter 4, as well as to reinforce your awareness of particular issues. Question 1 addresses the issue of the clubmen. Question 2, however, focusses on a different kind of source, and allows you to apply the skills of interpretation and evaluation to the visual sources with which this period is richly endowed. Considerations of space limit the number that can be provided in this volume, but wider reading will enable you to consider other examples.

1 Neutralism: the Clubmen
Carefully read the letter to Viscount Fairfax on page 94, the Articles of the Dorset and Wiltshire Clubmen on page 96, and John Morrill's comments on page 97. Answer the following questions.
a) What does the letter to Fairfax reveal about the impact of the war on non-combatants? (2 marks)
b) How does this help us to understand the actions of the Clubmen? (3 marks)
c) Do the Dorset and Wiltshire Articles suggest support for one side or the other? Explain your answer. (2 marks)
d) How far do the Clubmen represent anything more than war-weariness? (3 marks)
e) How far do these primary sources support Morrill's claims that the Clubmen were neutrals? (5 marks)
f) Using these sources and your wider knowledge of the period, explain the ways in which the Clubmen movements affected the outcome of the war. (10 marks)

2 Visual Sources.
The interpretation of visual sources is particularly reliant upon awareness and application of background knowledge (context). Consider the illustrations on page 46 (Chapter 3) and answer the following questions.
a) What point is being made in the picture of the Laudian Bishops? (2 marks)
b) Why are the Bishops shown in the centre and on the right presented as being much the same? (2 marks)
c) What would be the purpose of publishing such a picture? (3 marks)
d) What is being portrayed in the picture of the two preachers? (2 marks)
e) To what events and conditions operating in 1641 is the picture referring? (3 marks)
f) What would be the purpose of publishing such a picture? (3 marks)

In addition, visual sources need to be investigated in the light of who published them, when and why, in order to assess their reliability. Again, awareness of the context of events plays an important part in this process. Consider the illustrations of parliamentarian and royalist troops on page 95 and answer the following questions regarding each source.
g) What are the troops shown to be doing? (1 mark)
h) How might neutrals react to this behaviour? (2 marks)
i) Does your knowledge of the period suggest that this could be an accurate representation? (3 marks)
j) In the light of your responses, now explain which source you consider to be most reliable, which source you consider to be most useful, and why? (8 marks)

CHAPTER 6

The Emergence of the Radicals

By the end of 1646 it appeared that parliament would be able to achieve its objectives and establish a limited monarchy supported by a reformed Anglican Church. The king was defeated and the Scots had returned to Edinburgh, leaving the matter of a settlement in the hands of the English parliament. Popular war-weariness could be soothed by a return to normal government and a reduction of high war-time taxes. The governing class could rest secure in its rights and privileges under the Crown. But this did not happen. Instead, the ensuing year saw the parliament faced with army mutiny and the collapse of negotiations into a second Civil War. In May 1647 the army defied orders to disband, in June it seized the king and began independent political negotiations. In July and August a three-cornered struggle for power between king, parliament and army developed. At the same time, the army leaders were engaged in their own power struggle, for control of the army itself, in the face of radical demands for the forcible dissolution of parliament and its replacement by a democratically elected republic. The year ended in political deadlock, which was broken by the king's instigation of a Scottish invasion and a Second Civil War in 1648. When that was over, the full importance of the new political and religious forces which had emerged in 1647 would be revealed.

The following chapter seeks to explain the emergence of these new forces during the course of 1647, and to assess their impact on events. It begins with an examination of the origins of radical groups and their ideas, and traces their development to the end of 1646. This provides the context in which the search for a settlement in 1647 revealed their existence and and shaped their evolution. These events fall into three chronological sections leading up to the outbreak of the Second Civil War in early 1648. The first section demonstrates how parliament's initial actions in the spring of 1647 led to an army mutiny and considers the origins and nature of army resistance; the second traces the struggle for power between parliament and army in the summer of 1647 and explains the nature of divisions over the future settlement with the king; the third highlights radical development through explaining the Leveller challenge and its failure in the autumn of 1647. The chapter ends, therefore, with a reunited parliament and army facing the challenge of renewed Civil War, and assesses how far the situation had changed as a result of the emergence of radicalism as a political and religious force.

1 The Origins of Radicalism

The core and origin of this radicalism was religious. The Protestant faith, particularly in its puritan form, emphasised individual belief, active commitment, and a personal relationship with God. Encouraged to read and study the Bible, and told that the rules of true faith were contained therein, individual believers were led to develop their own interpretations of a book that was part history, part myth and part poetry. Believing themselves to be chosen by God as his people, some felt unable to remain within a Church which was only half-reformed by the Elizabethan Settlement of 1558-9, and were led, often by an inspirational preacher or minister, into the establishment of independent or separate congregations. Since these were illegal, and separation was, in itself, a subversive act, these congregations led a secretive and isolated existence; the effect of isolation and of continuing and enthusiastic internal debate was to encourage new and more unorthodox ideas to emerge. The Baptists, for example, had adopted the practice of adult, rather than infant baptism, as a commitment to church membership. Gifted members of such congregations were encouraged to debate with the minister (hence to question authority) and even to preach (officially the exclusive preserve of the educated, professional clergy). Thus traditional ideas of spiritual equality were given a new and practical form and expression. The General Baptists had even come to reject predestination itself, arguing that a loving God would open the gift of salvation to all who wished to receive it. In many ways and many forms the experience of religious separatism undermined and weakened the concepts of social hierarchy and obedience to authority upon which seventeenth-century society and government rested and relied.

The attack on the authority of the bishops in 1641 led to the collapse of censorship. With access to a free press, radical arguments and ideas could be expressed publicly and could be openly debated. Lay preachers appeared in London. The outbreak of war heightened visionary ideas of a struggle between good and evil, and the victories of parliament's armies encouraged the belief that God approved their cause. Separatist churches operated with increasing confidence, and little could be done in wartime conditions to control their activities. In 1641 the London General Baptists held a joint conference, and in 1643 seven churches of the London Particular Baptists issued a joint Confession of Faith. In 1644 the first Independent, or Congregational, Church was founded in Hull, followed by Canterbury in 1645. By 1646, there were six such churches in Yorkshire alone. Most ominous of all for worried conservatives, by 1644 these separatists were demanding that any religious settlement should officially and permanently grant them the right to worship as they chose. While the Independent ministers in the Westminster Assembly of Divines asked only for a limited toleration, others such as Roger Williams (who later founded the American colony of Rhode Island) were denying that government should have any role in religion, and questioning the existence of any state Church, especially one supported by tithes (a compulsory local tax of one tenth of produce or income, to be paid to the parish clergy).

By 1644, therefore, religious radicalism had begun to challenge the very foundations of society and to develop new political ideas and demands. For the most part these came as a response to practical needs. Denial of religious freedom in practice led to the formulation of arguments to justify it, and hence to theories about a wider range of rights and freedoms. In the same way, Presbyterian attacks on John Milton's ideas in favour of divorce led him to write and publish *The Areopagitica*, a passionately argued case for free speech and a free press. The number of separatists was always small, (a few hundred in 1644, probably no more than ten thousand at any time until the emergence of the Quakers in 1652) and the number of political radicals in their ranks even smaller, but the threat that they seemed to represent was enormous in conservative eyes. Moreover, by the end of 1646, two factors seemed to give real substance to their fears. The first was the emergence of a radical political movement in London in 1646, in the shape of the Leveller party; the second was the apparent strength of radical ideas within the New Model Army.

The Leveller party developed from the campaign for religious toleration which was under way in London by 1644. Its leading figures, John Lilburne, William Walwyn and Richard Overton, were all products of religious separatism. As an apprentice in London in the 1630s, Lilburne had attended the sermons of puritan preachers and had been prosecuted by the High Commission in 1638 for smuggling and distributing banned religious tracts. Whipped, pilloried and imprisoned, he had used his public notoriety to attack the power of the bishops to imprison people, and to assert his rights as a 'freeborn Englishman'. Released by the Long Parliament in 1641, he volunteered for parliament's forces in 1642, but left the army in 1644 in protest at the Solemn League and Covenant (the alliance with the Scots which included a promise to establish Presbyterianism in England). Returning to London, he seems to have joined a congregation of General Baptists, and was attracted to meetings of political radicals at the Whalebone Tavern, where campaigns for religious toleration were beginning to be orchestrated. There he made the acquaintance of the wealthy merchant William Walwyn, and the radical pamphleteer, Richard Overton. By 1645 the three had formed the core of a radical group arguing for complete freedom of belief and worship as a right for all.

By 1645 these radicals were well known for their views, and conservative enemies were eager to stop their activities. In July Lilburne was accused of slandering the Speaker of the House of Commons, William Lenthall, and imprisoned on parliament's orders. His response was to publish a pamphlet *England's Birthright Justified* in which he protested at being imprisoned without proper trial, and accused the House of tyranny. He developed the argument into a demand for social and legal equality. By July 1646 the Levellers as a group were sufficiently notorious to merit a special section in Thomas Edwards' *Gangraena*, a bitter attack upon various radical groups which sought to alert parliament to the danger that they represented. Lilburne was accused by the Presbyterian William Prynne of slander against the House of Lords. Called by the Lords to answer the charges, he stood at the bar of the House, refused to remove his hat, and harangued the Lords for their injustice in thus summoning him. He was once again imprisoned, but this led to a campaign by his wife and other Levellers for his release, in which Lilburne's experiences were used as the basis of demands for more wide-ranging political reform. Petitions, demonstrations and marches were organised in London, and pamphlets by Lilburne and others were published, setting out an increasingly comprehensive and coherent programme of political, legal and economic change. In a petition delivered to the Commons, entitled *A Remonstrance of Many Thousand Citizens* the Levellers claimed that the war had been waged for liberty, and that citizens should now be given their rights. The parliament was accused of being concerned only with its own interests. The argument drew together an attack on the monarchy, demands for political rights (including religious toleration) and a range of popular grievances over economic, social and legal inequality. It laid the basis for a wide-ranging programme of reform and a new form of government, based on a parliament elected by, and responsible to, the people as a whole.

While parliament might ignore the Leveller petitions and demonstrations, they could not but be concerned by the evidence of religious radicalism in the ranks of the New Model Army. Not only did the soldiers preach, pray and debate among themselves (with and without the help of their chaplains and ministers) but complaints from many parts of the country showed that they encouraged and protected civilian separatists wherever they went. The first Congregational Church in England, at Dagger Lane in Hull, was established and encouraged by the Independent minister, Philip Nye with the help of the garrison preacher, John Canne. Nor was this malign influence limited to the lower ranks - Cromwell himself and many other officers were known to regard a man's religious beliefs as his own private affair, and to have protected those of unorthodox or radical views from punishment or persecution. In 1645 the moderate Presbyterian minister, Richard Baxter, had visited the army at its quarters near Naseby and been appalled by what he found.

1 We that lived quietly in Coventry did keep to our old principles and thought all others had done so too, except a few very inconsiderable persons ... we believed that the war was only to save the Parliament and Kingdom from papists and delinquents, and to 5 remove the dividers, that the King might again return to his Parliament; and that no changes might be made in religion, but by the laws which had his free consent ... And when the court news-book told the world of the swarms of Anabaptists in our

armies, we thought it had been a mere lie, because it was not so
10 with us, nor in any of the garrison or county forces about us. But
when I came to the army among Cromwell's soldiers, I found a
new face of things which I never dreamt of: I heard the plotting
heads very hot upon that which intimated their intention to subvert
15 both Church and State. Independency and Anabaptristry were
most prevalent ... Abundance of the common troopers, and many
of the officers, I found to be honest, sober, orthodox men, and
others tractable, ready to hear the truth, and of upright intentions;
but a few proud, self-conceited, hot-headed sectaries had got into
20 the highest places, and were Cromwell's chief favourites, and by
their heat and activity bore down the rest, or carried them along
with them, and were the soul of the army ... I found that many
honest men of weak judgements and little acquaintance with such
matters, had been seduced into a disputing vein, and made it too
25 much of their religion to talk for this opinion and for that;
sometimes for State democracy and sometimes for Church
democracy.

It was hardly surprising that such an army should cause concern, which
grew as complaints multiplied throughout 1646. According to Thomas
Edwards,

1 The army that is so much spoken of upon all occasions in the news-
books, pulpits, conferences, to be Independent (though I conceive
upon good information, that upon a true muster of the whole,
commanders and common soldiers, there would not be found
5 above one in six of that way); yet of that army, called by the
sectaries, Independent, and of that part of it which truly is so, I do
not think there are 50 pure Independents, but higher flown, more
seraphical ... made up and compounded of Anabaptism,
Antinomianism [believing that those whom God had saved were
10 incapable of sin] Enthusiasm, Arminianism [believing that
salvation was open to all] Familism [believing that God existed
within all]; all these errors and more too sometimes meeting in the
same persons ...

His intemperate language and willingness to raise every possible
nightmare had its effect on MPs. With soldiers concerning themselves in matters of 'church democracy and state democracy' in
Baxter's words, it is not surprising that conservatives feared the
worst. That such radicals constituted a small minority, even within
the army, was less important and less influential than the fact that
they existed at all. It was therefore all the more important, in the
minds of many MPs, that a settlement with the king should be
concluded, which would restore the traditional structures and

controls provided by the partnership of monarchy and parliament.

2 The Parliamentary Search for Settlement

By the end of 1646, with the king effectively under house arrest at Holdenby in Northants. and the Scots paid off to return to Edinburgh, MPs were free to attend to the establishment of peace. While most MPs assumed that Charles would have to come to some agreement, however reluctantly, the old problem of trusting him to maintain it remained a serious obstacle. Parliamentary control of the armed forces and of the king's advisers would do much to overcome this, always assuming that Charles would be prepared to listen to their advice! An equally contentious area was the nature of the Church settlement. In 1645-6 the Westminster Assembly of Divines had finally issued a Directory of Worship, which instituted a mild form of Presbyterianism, and in some areas, such as London, this had been partially established in practice. However, when these schemes were put to the king in the form of the proposals presented to him at Newcastle, Charles made it perfectly clear that they were unacceptable. As long as he remained in Scottish hands, his attitude created the possibility that he might join with the

THE
World turn'd upfide down
OR,
A briefe defcription of the ridiculous Fafhions
of thefe diftracted Times.

By T.J. a well-willer to King, Parliament and Kingdom.

London : Printed for *John Smith*. 1 6 4 7.

The World Turned Upside Down, *the title page of an anti-radical tract published in 1646*

Covenanters to renew the war. Their insistence on rigid Presbyterianism in the Church was even less palatable to him; but their willingness to restore his political power might yet prove sufficiently attractive to persuade him to accept their religious goals in the hope of overturning them later when he had greater room for manoeuvre. Once he was in the hands of the English parliament, however, this danger receded, and the parliamentary leaders felt able to wait upon developments with the king while busying themselves with more immediate problems.

These revolved to a great extent around the instrument of their success, the New Model Army. In the first place, the army was expensive and the population was increasingly resentful of heavy taxation. The war-weariness of a nation which had borne unprecedented levels of expenditure, as well as destruction and the dislocation of trade, was a factor which parliament had to consider, especially as it might well operate in favour of the king. Now that the threat of renewed war had receded, it was natural that the remedy of disbanding the army should be considered. In addition, the army's reputation for political and religious radicalism horrified the majority of MPs. In 1644-5 the needs of war had seen the more radical MPs able to dominate the House of Commons, but the advent of peace had changed the situation. In order to make itself more fully representative of the political nation, parliament had held by-elections in the seats occupied by royalists. The hundred or so of these 'recruited' MPs elected in 1645 were mainly supporters of the war effort, but the further 135 elected in 1646 were largely concerned with the return of peace and 'normality', strengthening the conservative 'peace party' of the early war days. In this situation the peace leaders, Denzil Holles and Sir Philip Stapleton, had regained much of their earlier influence and they were eager to consolidate this and weaken the radicals by getting rid of their primary weapon, the army. It was therefore neither unreasonable nor surprising that they should seek both to solve parliament's financial problems and to rid themselves of an uncomfortable ally by proposing the disbandment of the army in early 1647.

This proposal was enthusiastically received by MPs, who voted in favour in February 1647. Most regiments were to be disbanded, but a few were invited to volunteer for service in Ireland, where a campaign to deal with the rebels of 1641 was at last under way. These were to have new officers, and those who had previously been excepted from the Self-Denying Ordinance (Cromwell and others such as his son-in-law, Henry Ireton, who had been 'recruited' in 1645-6) were to return to parliamentary duty. On the face of it these were reasonable measures, but it did not escape the notice of the troops that the officers they would lose were all sympathisers with Independent or sectarian religious views, and that their replacements were more orthodox in outlook. More seriously, the disbandment made no allowance for payment of the soldiers' arrears of pay, nor gave them indemnity from prosecution for acts carried out during the war. These were issues of great concern to the rank and file. Many had not received adequate pay for months, and it has been estimated that by the end of the war, parliament's various armies were owed something in the region of £3 million. Indemnity was also a serious matter. Already by early 1647 there were reports of ex-troopers being hanged for theft as a result of requisitioning horses under orders during the war. Without legal protection from parliament, many of parliament's troops would be at risk of such prosecutions.

In March, therefore, the army petitioned their General, Sir Thomas Fairfax, to seek changes on their behalf. At this point the petitions were almost exclusively concerned with pay and indemnity rather than political or religious matters, and there is little doubt that concessions on these issues could have secured the peaceful disbandmant of many regiments. Holles, however, had little sympathy for military concerns, and the death of the Earl of Essex in September 1646 had robbed him of expert military advice. He dismissed arguments that parliament could afford some payment of arrears, and persuaded the House of Commons to publish a Declaration of Dislike on 30 March, declaring the petitioners to be 'enemies of the state and disturbers of the public peace'. It was a serious misjudgement, and infuriated the soldiers, who had fought for the cause of parliament and considered themselves worthy of its gratitude rather than such condemnation. In April a number of cavalry regiments (always better educated than the infantry, many of whom were conscripted men) elected Agents or 'Agitators' to represent their views and these joined with the junior officers to voice the army's discontent. Again, there was little reference to religion at this point, but it is noticeable that a number of the representatives were Baptists, although this may only indicate that they were among the more articulate of the troopers, having experience of debate and public speaking in their religious meetings. Whether or not religious matters were a major cause of concern at first, they were to become increasingly important in the months that followed.

Despite appeals by Cromwell and other MPs who were sympathetic to the soldiers' claims, the conservatives pressed ahead, ordering the disbandment to take place on 1 June. On 31 May two regiments mutinied, and the crisis rapidly came to a head, despite concessions from parliament. The soldiers were now convinced that the conservative MPs intended to betray the cause for which they had fought, and conclude an agreement with the king that would sacrifice their political and religious liberties. A meeting of the Agitators ordered Cornet Joyce to secure control of the king, probably in order to prevent any such agreement. On 3 June Joyce met Cromwell in London, and probably informed him of the army's intention. On 4 June he removed the king from Holdenby House, and took him to the army's headquarters at Newmarket. On 5 June the regiments met in a general rendezvous and accepted the *Solemn Engagement* by which the army declared its refusal to disband until a just settlement which guaranteed the rights of 'freeborn Englishmen' was obtained. The *Solemn Engagement* also established a General Council of officers and agitators to co-ordinate the army's campaign. The same day Cromwell left London and rejoined the army, making public his support for its cause. Finally, on 14 June the army published its *Representation*, in which its political programme was oulined and its political intervention justified.

Written by Henry Ireton, who was to become the army's most influential political thinker, the *Representation* demanded a purge of corrupt MPs who were willing to betray parliament's cause, naming eleven conservatives including Holles and Stapleton. The present parliament was to be dissolved as soon as practicable, and future parliaments should be of fixed duration. The Church was to be reformed, and toleration granted to 'tender consciences' - those, like the Independents and Baptists, who believed that the state Church was not a 'true' church of believers, or objected to some of its practices, and preferred to worship in their own voluntary congregations. The document represented the emergence of the army as a political force, both in its radical demands, and in their justification. 'We are not', it declared, 'a mere mercenary army', but a body of volunteers who had responded to parliament's call to defend liberty. As such, the soldiers had a right to participate in establishing the settlement for which they had fought, and for which their comrades had died. Whatever settlement might emerge from this crisis, it was clear that it could no longer be concluded by king and parliament alone - a new and radical element had emerged onto the political scene.

a) The Politicisation of the Army

It is important to analyse how and why this political evolution of the army had occurred. There is no doubt that the misjudgements of parliamentary conservatives had been largely responsible for the first stirrings of resistance, and that many soldiers were, and remained, motivated first and foremost by material concerns such as pay and arrears. Historians of the army, from C.H.Firth to Mark Kishlansky and Austin Woolrych, have shown clearly that the New Model was not made up of political and religious visionaries, but contained many conscripted or mercenary troops for whom the military life was a profession rather than a crusade. Nevertheless, the speed with which political and religious demands were formulated, the coherence of the arguments and programme put forward and the determination and confidence displayed, by troopers and junior officers as well as the army leaders, suggests that the crisis arose from something more (and more deep-seated) than arrears and ingratitude.

The issue of how and why the army emerged as a political force has been fiercely debated among historians. Those who see 1648-9 as a year of revolution have stressed the emergence of radical ideas and the influence of the Levellers, while the 'revisionist' school of Kishlansky and others has emphasised the importance of material issues and the misjudgements of the conservatives. It is clear that both elements played a part - what is at issue is their relative importance, and that must be carefully weighed against the evidence. On the one hand, there is no doubt that the behaviour of parliament was provocative, and that the material concerns of the soldiers were both widespread and real. There is little evidence of Leveller involvement until the crisis was well under way, in May 1647. In that month new Agitators were elected who included some troopers - Edward Sexby, William Allen and Captain White - who are known to have had Leveller connections. In the same month came the first clear expression of religious grievances and a demand for religious liberty. The army's *Engagement* of 5 June uses a typically Leveller reference to 'freeborn Englishmen', although it was actually written by the officer and MP, Henry Ireton. What is suggested by this evidence is that the crisis was created by conservative mistakes, and that the Levellers saw in the discontented soldiers potential allies for their cause.

However, if we consider why the conservatives made such misjudgements, the perspective is somewhat altered. It was the existence of radicalism in the army, at least in religion, which led conservatives to be anxious to dispose of it so quickly. The likelihood is that conservative fears were exaggerated, that radicals were few (as Baxter implied), but that they were not imaginary. Put together, the radical publications of the war years, including parliament's own appeals for resistance to tyranny, the spread of separatist congregations and the existence of religious radicals in the army do suggest that a new factor of some significance had emerged by 1646, which parliament's perceptions of a satisfactory settlement failed to take into account. The speed with which the army produced effective spokesmen, and the failure of parliament's concessions on pay and indemnity at the end of May indicate that for some, at least, the crisis reflected deeper concerns. If Leveller influence became important, it was because some common ideas, especially regarding religious freedom, had already taken root among the regiments. Moreover, what made the army so effective so quickly was the agreement achieved between officers and men, in which common concerns with political and religious issues played a vital role. While conservative mistakes undoubtedly dictated the shape and timing of the crisis, its origins lay in the impact and experience of war and the separate radical agenda that had developed among a small, but significant, minority of the population.

This argument is further strengthened by consideration of the way in which the army justified its political intervention. Ireton argued that the soldiers had fought for a cause in which they believed. They might not have been elected to represent the people in the matter of settlement, but they did represent the people of God, and God had publicly blessed their cause. His argument is clearly influenced by a belief, widespread in this period, in God's Providence as the deciding factor in the affairs of men. This belief, particularly strong among those of puritan inclinations, emphasised God's direct control of events and asserted that God decided whether or not individuals should succeed in their endeavours. Thus the defeat of the king signified God's approval of parliament's cause, and the successes of the New Model meant that God had chosen and approved the army as the instrument of his Will. Hence the military had a special right, and duty, to participate in deciding what kind of settlement should emerge from the struggle.

It is inconceivable, therefore, that the behaviour of the army in the spring of 1647 can be understood without reference to its religion and the resulting interpretation of its wartime experience. The army was not an army of Saints, but there were Saints within it who believed in their duty to fight for God's cause, and who would never have stood by while parliament apparently betrayed it. Thus the conditions existing at the end of the war in 1646, which included the development of political and religious radicalism, made some kind of crisis among the supporters of parliament probable if not inevitable. The errors made by conservatives in response to these conditions ensured that the army would be united in this crisis, and that it would initiate a struggle in which parliament would be the loser.

3 Army, Parliament and King, June–November 1647

With the king safely in their hands and the soldiers united behind them, the army leaders now sought to establish an acceptable settlement. The key figures among the Grandees (the name increasingly applied to the senior army officers) were Oliver Cromwell and his son-in-law, Henry Ireton. They were both radical in religion, and therefore sympathetic to appeals for toleration. They were also members of the lesser gentry, sharing the belief in a hierarchical society and in the existing social and economic structures that was common to the ruling class. Of the two, Ireton was the better theoretician, but Cromwell approached the business of settlement with practical common sense, a desire for compromise and a sense of social justice which contributed a good deal to the proposals that emerged. In the 1630s he had sought to protect the rights of fen dwellers in East Anglia against the 'improvers' and their drainage schemes, not because he opposed the schemes, but because he believed that the dispossessed should be adequately compensated. Years later, as Lord Protector, he would claim that he was 'not wedded to forms' of government, and the same was true of his religious and social attitudes. His reputation for protecting religious radicals arose largely from the fact that his judgement of the soldiers who served him was based on their military merit, with little regard for their social origins or religious views. Hence his well-known praise of 'plain, russet-coated captains'. Equally, in defending an Anabaptist from persecution by the Presbyterian Major-General Crawford, he argued that a man's religious views should be a private matter - 'the State, in choosing men to serve them, takes no notice of their opinions'.

The settlement proposed by these men, with the help of the junior officer John Lambert, was a masterpiece of compromise. It was more generous to the king than parliament's Newcastle Propositions, offering the return of his legislative veto, control of the militia after ten years, and the restoration of bishops in the Church, albeit without coercive powers. Liberty of conscience would be granted to all but Catholics. Only five royalists were to be excepted from a general pardon. In addition, the proposals included provision for social and legal reform, parliamentary elections every two years, and a redistribution of parliamentary seats on the basis of taxation. Historians (particularly historians of the Levellers) have seen Leveller influence in these latter provisions, and this may well have been the case, but there is nothing in the proposals that did not accord comfortably with the attitudes and practice of Cromwell both before and after 1647. (For evaluation of these and other peace proposals presented to Charles, a Comparative Chart has been included as an Appendix, preceding the Chronological Table provided at the end of this book).

Under the title of the *Heads of the Proposals* these ideas were presented to the king on 2 August. By now the crisis had moved on to divide parliament itself, and the army was approaching London. The move had been sparked off by conservatives in the city. Furious at the army's resistance to disbandment and its demand that Holles and ten other MPs should be impeached, the city merchants and clergy offered loans to pay for disbandment and the London militia to defend parliament. Dislike of religious radicalism, disorder and continuing expense provided a powerful motivation, and the increasingly royalist London mobs were encouraged to demonstrate for a settlement with the king. In July the mob invaded parliament itself, and fifty-eight MPs, including the Speakers of both Houses, fled to the army for safety. With this stamp of authority and legitimacy, Fairfax began a slow march on London, the city militia melted away, and the eleven MPs named by the army for impeachment fled. On 4 August the army entered London unopposed.

This parliamentary crisis of July undermines any assumptions that 1647 revealed a simple division between army and parliament, suggesting rather that parliament itself was divided over the nature of the settlement that was desired. Throughout the spring the initiative had been held by the conservative group gathered around Denzil Holles and the Committee for Disbandment who met at Derby House. There is little doubt that the majority of MPs were content to support this group, but there were some who were more sympathetic to the army's aspirations, and who shared their religious views and distrust of the king.

Because the conservatives broadly supported parliament's Presbyterian scheme of church reform, and the opposing minority were sympathetic to a measure of religious toleration, they have been labelled political Presbyterians and Independents, but such labels disguise as much as they reveal. In the first place, the groups did not really conform to these religious divisions. Many conservatives, like Holles, could happily accept bishops in the Church, provided their power was reduced and parliament's supremacy asserted. In contrast, some religious Presbyterians, such as Zouch Tate and Isaac Penington, aligned themselves with the army. Secondly, it is erroneous to visualise clear-cut groups at all. Most MPs behaved as individuals, attempting to pick their way through a confused and confusing clash of ideas and personalities, to find a settlement for problems with which parliaments had never previously had to grapple. However, there were two small groups of parliamentarians who shared beliefs and personal links. One centred on Holles, Essex and Stapleton, and the other on Vane, St.John, Haselrig, Cromwell and Lord Saye and Sele. They corresponded to some degree with the old 'peace' and 'war' parties, and they were divided less by religion than by a wider vision of settlement and how it was to be achieved. At different times and in different situations, the majority of uncommitted MPs accepted the lead of one or other group, as seemed appropriate.

For the Holles group, the restoration of order took priority - hence they supported 'Presbyterianism' because it seemed to offer the best prospect of an effective state Church which could fulfil its traditional role of maintaining social and political authority over the people. They regarded the king as the lynch-pin of order, and were willing to make significant concessions in order to restore him to his place. Hence the term 'conservative' seems most appropriate to describe them. We cannot, however, use the neatly opposed 'radical', let alone 'revolutionary', to describe the other party. Its members' attitudes were characterised by a deeper suspicion of the king and a greater determination to achieve guarantees of political and religious rights, rather than by an entirely different concept of what a settlement should be. If there was any religious characteristic common to the group, it tended to be a concern with religious, or spiritual matters, rather than a particular form of religion or membership of any denomination. Hence a church which could uphold social cohesion was essential, but no more so than 'liberty for tender consciences' within or alongside it. It could be said that the main difference between the two groups lay in their sense of priorities rather than in any clash of fundamental political vision.

In this situation, the army mutinies consolidated conservative support and posed a problem for their sympathisers. MPs like Cromwell and Vane believed in the rights and authority of parliament, whilst sympathising with the soldiers' aspirations. In the end, Cromwell and other officers placed themselves at the head of the army revolt in order to maintain its unity and to exercise a restraining influence. Without a united army, their opportunity to influence the settlement would rest on their weak position as a parliamentary minority. In July, however, it was the conservative mobs in London who posed the threat to order and the rights of parliament. Hence many uncommitted MPs joined those who took refuge with the army, and gave a legitimate reason for Fairfax's march on the city. What the divisions in parliament in the summer of 1647 most clearly indicate is the fluidity of the situation at this point. Its future development would depend very much on the nature of any agreement that the army leaders hoped to negotiate with the king.

Such hopes were now to be disappointed by the king himself. Charles had watched his enemies fall out, and had drawn the erroneous but appealing conclusion that he could use their differences for his own ends. This was not an unnatural response, reinforced by the fact that the Heads were a significant improvement on parliament's earlier proposals. Moreover, there were genuine difficulties for Charles. Authoritarian and wedded to belief in his divine right, he would be reluctant to surrender control of religious belief to the extent that was suggested, let alone control of the militia. Derek Hirst has suggested that he would have found it hard to abandon his friends (the five excepted royalists), although Charles treatment of those, such as Prince Rupert, who had served him in war indicates that his conscience could be somewhat elastic in such matters. Most important, however, Charles did not believe that he needed to come to terms at this time. The major miscalculation of all those who sought to achieve a settlement with Charles was to assume that he would accept his military defeat as final. For Cromwell and the army, it was God's verdict on the conflict. For Charles it was a temporary setback in his struggle to defeat a rebellion. He was the king, and there could be no settlement without him. He had other kingdoms - Scotland and Ireland - on whom he might legitimately call. If his enemies were falling out among themselves, he could afford to wait until one or other of them came round to his way of thinking. He therefore delayed his answer to the army's proposals and awaited parliament's reaction. Disappointing as this may have been for the army leaders, they had little time to dwell on it, since they were already engaged in a separate struggle for control of the army itself.

4 The Leveller Challenge, July-November 1647

By early June 1647 it was clear that the Leveller movement had established at least a foothold within the army. Parliament's rejection of their plans had encouraged the Leveller leaders to look for alternative sources of support, and the discontents of the army rank and file provided fertile ground for their arguments. The army General Council provided a platform for Leveller demands and, although John Lilburne remained in prison throughout the summer of 1647, he was able to exercise an influence through Agitators like Edward Sexby and civilian contacts like John Wildman, a London Leveller who played a significant part in drafting the Agitators' declarations and claims. He bore the title of 'Major' Wildman, but there is no record of his having served in the New Model. By the early summer of 1647 Leveller ideas had been concentrated into a demand for the dissolution of the Long Parliament and its replacement by a new Assembly, elected on a wide franchise, and the leaders looked to the army to carry out the task. The Grandees' refusal to carry out such a coup, and their march on London to restore parliament's independence frustrated the radicals, and the continuing negotiations with the king provoked suspicions of a deal which would leave the Levellers isolated.

In an attempt to regain the initiative and refocus the army's efforts, Wildman issued a new political declaration, *The Case of the Army Truly Stated* in October, and demanded that the General Council debate it. The document summarised the soldiers' grievances and wove them into a wider case for political reform based on a genuinely representative parliament. While it did not necessarily call for the removal of the king, power was deemed to be derived from the people, and their elected representatives were clearly regarded as being superior to any monarch. In order to exercise control of their representatives, the people were to have new elections every two years, and parliamentary seats were to be based on population. This clearly implied something akin to manhood suffrage. Government was to be further limited by certain fundamental laws, which guaranteed political rights and liberties, including religious toleration.

The *Case of the Army* did not constitute a clear and coherent set of constitutional laws, but it did advance revolutionary and effectively democratic theories of government. Re-drafted into the *Agreement of the People* for debate in the army council, it drew on a number of sources. Parliament's own arguments about the 'ancient and fundamental' constitution, the imposition of the 'Norman yoke' of monarchy and the rule of law formed a base. But where parliament had claimed authority for itself to resist tyranny as a 'lesser magistrate', the Levellers had gone directly to the source of power, the people. The revolutionary step that they had taken in arguing that all people were capable of exercising political rights, owed much to the experience of the separatist churches, where spiritual equality and rights of debate had extended beyond the governing class. Most significant, where other churches had demanded these rights and freedoms for God's people, as privileges for the Saints, the Levellers accepted the General Baptist claim of salvation for all. Thus, if all were capable of salvation because God had given them the capacity to accept faith through human reason, then all were capable of exercising that reason in human affairs. Religious belief and experience had led them to a basic theory of human rights.

Extracts from the *Agreement of the People*

1 Having by our late labours and hazards made it appear to the world
at how high a rate we value our just freedom, and God having so far
owned our cause as to deliver the enemies thereof into our hands,
we do now hold ourselves bound in mutual duty to each other to
5 take the best care we can for the future ... Since, therefore, our
former oppressions and scarce-yet-ended troubles have been
occasioned, either by want of frequent national meetings in
Council, or by rendering those meetings ineffectual, we are fully
agreed and resolved to provide that hereafter our representatives
10 be neither left to an uncertainty for the time nor made useless to
the ends for which they are intended. In order whereunto we
declare:

That the people of England, being at this day very unequally
distributed by Counties, Cities and Boroughs for the election of
15 their deputies in Parliament, ought to be more indifferently
proportioned according to the number of the inhabitants ...

That to prevent the many inconveniences apparently arising from
the long continuance of the same persons in authority, this present
Parliament be dissolved upon the last day of September ... 1648.

20 That the people do choose themselves a Parliament once in two
years ...

That the power of this and all future Representatives of this Nation
is inferior only to those who choose them, and doth extend ... to
whatsoever is not expressly or impliedly reserved by the
represented to themselves: Which are as followeth,

25 1 That matters of religion and the ways of God's worship are not at
all entrusted by us to any human power, because therein we cannot
remit or exceed title of what our consciences dictate to be the mind
of God without wilful sin: nevertheless, the public way of
instructing the nation (so it be not compulsive) is referred to their
discretion.

30 2 That the matter of impresting and constraining any of us to serve
in the wars is against our freedom; and therefore we do not allow it
...

4 That in all laws made or to be made, every person may be bound
alike ...

5 That as the laws ought to be equal, so they must be good, and not
35 evidently destructive to the safety and well-being of the people ...

These things we declare to be our native rights ...

The Grandees were repelled by such revolutionary ideas. However, they had little choice but to allow the debate. In late October and early November the Army Council met in Putney Church, where Agitators and some officers spoke in favour of the Agreement, while Ireton led the challenge against it. The records of the debate are incomplete, but it is clear that it came to revolve mainly around the issue of the franchise, with Ireton arguing strongly in favour of the representation of property and interests rather than people. Cromwell's role was to contain the hostility of the debate, and seek above all to protect the unity of the army. It is difficult to know what the outcome would have been - certain of Ireton's criticisms were later accepted by the Levellers when they reduced the right to vote to all free men, removing the rights of servants, wage labourers and paupers - but the argument did appear to be going the Levellers' way when the whole procedure was brought to an abrupt end. On 11 November the king escaped from army custody, and made his way to Carisbrooke Castle on the Isle of Wight.

The king's escape was undoubtedly timely from the point of view of the Grandees. His greater freedom and easier access to France or other foreign help raised the possibility of renewed war, and gave Fairfax

Seventeenth-century print, believed to be of the Army Council at the Putney Debates. Note that the officers are sitting, while the Levellers and Agitators stand

reason to restore military discipline. An attempt by the Levellers and Agitators to have the army drawn up in a general rendezvous (where they hoped to offer it the *Agreement)* was defeated by Cromwell, who called three separate rendezvous to gather the troops together. The first, held at Corkbush Field near Ware in Hertfordshire, saw an abortive mutiny led by the regiment of Colonel Robert Lilburne, which was quickly suppressed when Cromwell rode in amongst the troops. Three troopers were arrested, and one shot - an indication of how limited and short-lived the mutiny was. The fury of the Levellers was vented in attacks upon the Grandees, but their position was weak. With the threat, and then the reality, of a second civil war, they could hardly justify attacking the generals upon whose efforts the safety of parliament and the cause depended. By the time the war was over, the political scene had changed. Although the Grandees concluded a brief alliance with the Levellers in the autumn of 1648, they were again outmanoeuvred. A council of officers rejected a second version of the Agreement in December, and offered its own revised draft to parliament, where it was simply laid aside. In 1649 the king was executed, and the monarchy abolished without any reference to Leveller ideas. Later attempts to subvert the army in 1649 led to the crushing of a Leveller mutiny at Burford, and the disintegration of the movement. Although it was unclear in 1647, the defeat of the Levellers at Putney had meant the effective end of Leveller influence.

What, then was the significance of the Leveller intervention in 1647? Despite the claims of the Leveller leaders, and of sympathetic historians, it is unlikely that they ever enjoyed widespread support. As a political party they built up a membership of several hundred in London, and were capable of organising demonstrations involving several thousands. They undoubtedly had some influence in the army, and were able to pressurise and complicate the position of the Grandees. The king's escape eased Cromwell's difficulties in this area, allowing him to end the debates and restore military discipline. Some historians of the Levellers have even suggested that he organised the escape himself, for this very purpose, although there is only circumstantial evidence to support such a claim. Nevertheless, the ease with which discipline was restored and the Levellers outflanked suggests that their support was always limited, and dependent upon the particular circumstances of 1647. Outside London, they made little impact. It was the concentration of Leveller support in the political capital, combined with the coincidental divisions of parliament and army, that gave the party its influence at this time.

Nevertheless, the Levellers do have significance for the ideas that they developed and made public. Among the dozens of Leveller pamphlets published between 1646 and 1649, it is easy to point to weaknesses and inconsistencies. Leveller ideas were being developed partly as a vision of the future inspired by an unprecedented upheaval in society, partly as a political programme for immediate adoption, and partly as a propaganda campaign in a bitter power struggle. In these circumstances it is not surprising that their ideas and plans lacked a measure of coherence. What is therefore significant is not the fact that some ideas were impractical, nor that some changed or were abandoned, but that in the context of the seventeenth century they were formulated at all. Drawing upon widely accepted beliefs, religious enthusiasm and personal experience, they enunciated theories of democratic government and personal rights and freedoms which would never entirely disappear. The fact of their existence is evidence of the revolutionary nature of events in this period, even if it was a revolution conducted by a minority, and doomed to failure.

5 Conclusion - The Emergence of the Radicals

The emergence and evolution of political and religious radicalism in 1646-7 was clearly not the sole reason for the failure to find a settlement after the first Civil War. That failure owed as much to the inflexible demands made by parliament and probably more to the attitude and beliefs of the king. However, the development of new demands within the army did introduce new complexities, and did encourage Charles's hopes by dividing his enemies. Yet it is doubtful whether this had great significance in the outcome of events. The actions and attitudes that Charles had taken up since succeeding to the throne in 1625 all point to an inflexibility which would have led him to reject any settlement that parliament could have accepted, with or without divisions in the parliamentary ranks. Nor were those divisions serious enough to afford him a real prospect of reversing the military outcome of the war. The speed and effectiveness with which parliament and army reunited in 1648 meant that by late summer the king was again facing defeat.

This did not, however, mean that the differences between the aims and aspirations of the radicals in the army and the conservatives in parliament were short-lived or insignificant. The emergence of radicalism reflected important forces in English society, which had been developing and evolving since the reign of Elizabeth. While it is true that radical ideas influenced only a small minority of the population, and had been able to spread only because of the conditions and impact of civil war, they were, nevertheless, a logical outcome of a century of religious development in England. Once a minority had begun to challenge the authority of the Church and to question the role of the State in religion, issues were raised which could not simply be ignored. The attempt to do so in early 1647 had sparked off the very crisis that the conservatives had sought to avoid. The political and social aspirations of the Levellers could be contained with relative ease, because seventeenth-century England lacked the economic and social structure as well as the communications which would allow them to establish widespread support. Religious enthusiasm, however, was a more dangerous force, since it cut across class barriers. Thus the events of 1647 created a new, and potentially revolutionary, political element in a united army, which claimed a role in the shaping of government and justified it by the will of God. They were capable of genuinely revolutionary solutions to the problems of settlement when the search was renewed in the autumn of 1648.

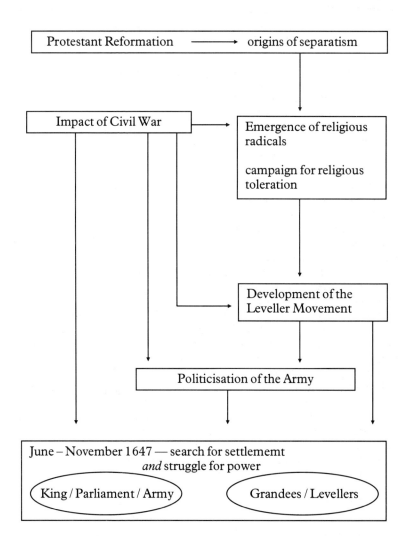

Summary - The Emergence of the Radicals

Making notes on 'The Emergence of the Radicals'

The structure of the chapter is clearly indicated by the headings included, and these will provide an overall structure for note-making. As in previous chapters, you will find it useful to devise sub-headings, based on the key points within each section. For example, the section on the Origins of Radicalism could be sub-divided into:

1. The nature of Protestant ideas
2. The development of separatism
3. The effects of crisis, 1641-4
4. The Levellers and their ideas
5. The New Model Army.

This model should be followed for the other sections, with sub-sections being devised as appropriate.

While the structure of the argument is clearly set out, the events of this period are both complex and important. You are therefore advised to take careful note of the dates that are provided, so that you can establish a clear chronological sequence - without this, you will not have a clear understanding of how the situation developed. You might find the Chronological Table on pages 151-154 helpful here.

Answering essay questions on 'The Emergence of the Radicals'

There are a number of possible questions which can be answered by drawing on the factors outlined above. For example, the central theme of why Radical groups emerged draws on both the events of the Civil War period and the earlier development of Protestant and Puritan beliefs. It can be argued that the nature of Protestantism provided the basic conditional factors leading to separatism and potentially radical ideas, while the breakdown of censorship, the upheaval of Civil War and the New Model Army enabled radicalism to emerge as a powerful force at this time. Similar questions can be asked about the rise, and failure, of the Levellers. From a different angle, the quarrels between parliament and army, and the behaviour of the king raise questions about the failure to negotiate a settlement and the role of radical forces in this failure as compared to the mistakes of the parliamentarians and the intransigence of the king. The material contained in this chapter can also be utilised in other, more wide-ranging essays - such as why parliament won the war and lost the peace. In addition, of course, this material is essential for explaining the execution of the king - which is discussed in the next chapter.

Look at the following questions.

1. Why did political and religious radicalism develop during the Civil War?

2. Why did parliament fail to establish an effective settlement after the First Civil War?
3. Why did the Levellers fail?
4. How far was the failure to find a settlement after the first Civil War the result of the attitudes and actions of Charles I?
5. Why did parliament win the war and lose the peace?

As described on page 101, you should begin to construct responses to such essay questions by defining the factors involved as either *conditional* or *contingent,* and preparing an outline essay plan on that basis. An essential element of a good essay is the need to assess the relative importance of the factors that combined to bring about a particular event or outcome. It is not enough simply to assert the importance of one or other factor - it has to be argued on the basis of evidence. One way of doing this that has been suggested is by looking at the relative roles of *conditional* and *contingent* factors (see pages 101-102). Another is by considering whether the absence of a particular factor would have changed the outcome - in other words, whether that particular factor was *necessary* for the event to take place. For example, the origins of religious radicalism lay in Protestant beliefs and the supremacy of the Bible. However, until the crisis of 1641 and the Civil War brought about the collapse of censorship and social control, separatist groups were small, isolated and often short-lived. Thus the wartime freedom can be seen as necessary for the development of radicalism. The spread of separatism was encouraged by the existence and mobility of the New Model Army, and undoubtedly by its victories, which seemed to indicate God's approval of the army and its cause, but it is likely that separatism would have developed a significant base even without this. Thus it can be said that Protestantism and the breakdown of controls were *necessary,* and *sufficient* to explain the emergence of radicalism, which was accelerated and intensified by the activities of the New Model Army and the victories of the parliamentary cause.

1. Plan an outline response to each of the essay questions listed above by identifying the factors involved and defining the role of each factor.
2. Use the idea of *necessary* and *sufficient* causes to explain the relative importance of the factors that you have outlined. (This could usefully be done in discussion with a group or partner).
3. Choose one essay to plan and write, utilising the ideas that you have considered and discussed.

Source-based questions on *'The Emergence of the Radicals'*

1 Conservative Fears
Carefully read the accounts of the army given by Baxter on pages 107-108 and Edwards on page 108. Answer the following questions.

a) In what ways do Baxter and Edwards agree about radicalism in the army? (3 marks)
b) What differences are there between their accounts? Explain the differences. (4 marks)
c) Does the fact that they are in broad agreement make their evidence reliable? Explain your answer. (4 marks)
d) Use these accounts, interpreted in the context of your wider knowledge, to summarise the religious state of the New Model Army. (4 marks)

Now consider the illustration *The World Turned Upside Down* on page 109.

e) What message is the person who produced the illustration attempting to communicate? (2 marks)
f) How far does the illustration substantiate the claims of Baxter and Edwards? (3 marks)
g) What do you consider to be the extent and significance of the conservative fears suggested by this evidence? (5 marks)

2 Radical Ideas

Carefully read the extracts from the *Agreement of the People* on page 119. Answer the following questions.

a) What are the main political principles expressed in the document? (4 marks)
b) What provision is made for religion and the Church? (2 marks)
c) In what ways did the Levellers seek to limit the power of government? (2 marks)
d) The document illustrates the theory of the 'sovereignty of the people'. What does this mean? How is it expressed in the *Agreement?* (4 marks)
e) Identify the similarities and differences between these plans and government in Britain today. (3 marks)
f) Cromwell and Ireton sympathised with religious radicals and their desire for some measure of religious toleration. Why then did they oppose and ultimately destroy the Levellers? (5 marks)
g) 'The Levellers failed because they were ahead of their time.' How valid is this comment? (10 marks)

CHAPTER 7

The Execution of the King, 1648-9

Charles I was executed on 30 January, 1649. He died a martyr at the hands of the army and a minority of MPs, against the will of the English people. In order to make this possible, parliament had been purged in early December 1648, with approximately 186 MPs forcibly excluded and another 45 imprisoned. A further 169 chose to be absent from the House until the execution had been carried out, although over 80 resumed attendance during the month of February 1649 and thus participated in the formal abolition of the monarchy and House of Lords in March. Only 71 of approximately 500 members of the Commons actively participated in the king's trial and execution, and of the 135 men named to be judges in the special High Court on 1 January, over half, including Sir Thomas Fairfax, refused to serve.

It is clear, therefore, that this was not the outcome sought by the majority of those who had fought against the king - yet it was the outcome of the Civil Wars. Even if these events are defined as the acts of a minority, as the description above suggests, it is necessary to explain why even a minority were prepared to bring an anointed monarch, God's representative on earth, to public trial and execution, and how they were in a position to do so. If we also consider why the majority did not share this determination, we may be able to highlight the importance of particular factors, and perhaps to understand why the 'revolution' thus enacted proved ultimately to be unsuccessful.

The following chapter approaches these issues in two ways. The first section traces the main events of 1648-9 to demonstrate how and why a minority of MPs, backed by the power of the army, brought the king to trial and execution. This is followed by a study guide, suggesting how you might construct effective notes on this material, and using source-based questions to explore some ideas more fully. The second section then focusses on the key question of why Charles was executed in 1649, and draws on both the material and the methodology outlined in earlier chapters to construct a response. This is intended to demonstrate the use of the methodological tools that have been introduced and developed through the different study guides, and to enable you to develop your own responses to a number of possible essay questions on this topic.

1 The Second Civil War and the Execution of the King

Militarily, the Second Civil War was of little significance. The 'rebel' forces fell into three main groups with little in common other than a dislike of the existing central authority and its policies. Among ex-parliamentarians as well as royalists there was a desire for a return to normal and familiar forms of government and resentment of the county committees and their ordinances. In Canterbury in December 1647 the parliamentary ordinance against the celebration of Christmas led to riots. When parliament, reacting to the king's Engagement with the Scots, passed a vote of No Further Addresses (to the king) in January 1648, outraged gentry organised local petitions calling for a treaty with the king and the disbandment of the army. In the spring of 1648 these local resentments led to disturbances in London and Norwich and outright rebellion in Kent, Essex, South Wales and in sections of the navy. The parliamentarian supporters who led these outbreaks were seeking to influence the decisions of parliament rather than to restore the king on his own terms, and the half-heartedness of their campaigns meant that they were quickly dealt with once the army stirred itself in April. More genuinely royalist were the cavalier risings in Cornwall, Yorkshire and Wales, but the majority of ex-royalists were unwilling or unable to react in support. Only in Wales and in Essex, where the royalists capitalised on the rebellion of ex-parliamentarians to seize control of Colchester, did lasting campaigns result. Colchester was besieged by Fairfax for several months, while Cromwell led a detachment of the New Model into Wales.

The third element of the king's support, the Scottish army, entered England in July. Despite the Engagement, the Scots had been slow to raise forces, and were further hampered by quarrels between the nobility and the Kirk (Presbyterian Church, whose ministers had great influence in the Scottish Lowlands). Dogged by bad weather in England, the Scottish army struggled into Lancashire where they were harried and delayed by Colonel John Lambert's Yorkshire troops. In August Cromwell, having completed his task of suppressing the South Wales rebels, turned north to catch the Scots at Preston on 17 August. In two days he had destroyed their much larger force, bringing any significant royalist threat to an end. Although the siege of Colchester lasted another 10 days, and mopping up operations in Yorkshire occupied Cromwell himself until early December, the war had effectively finished before August was ended.

These events were of enormous political significance. On the one hand, the conservative case for a compromise peace was enormously strengthened, while on the other, the army became adamantly opposed to any such treaty. Although the rebellions had been ill-coordinated and ineffective, the widespread unrest revealed popular dislike of parliament's attempts to reform religion and manners and the resentment of the local elites against its control of local government. The title of John Morrill's study of localism in the civil wars, *The Revolt of the Provinces,* was inspired by the Second Civil War. The House of Commons responded by rescinding its vote of No Addresses, allowing negotiations to be re-opened with the king, and in June 1648 the eleven conservative members whose impeachment the army had demanded in 1647 re-took their seats. In September, the House despatched commissioners to meet with the king on the Isle of Wight. When the army had done its work for parliament's safety, there was every prospect that its interests would be sacrificed in a new treaty between the parliamentary majority and the king.

However, the army had no intention of allowing this to happen, and it is at this point that the full significance of its politicisation in 1647 becomes apparent. In that year reservations regarding the king's reliability in any settlement had been made public, and the army had declared its right to a voice in any political settlement. Now it intended to exercise that right. The Second Civil War had greatly strengthened its position on both issues. Charles's negotiations with the Scots, his secret Engagement, his willingness to see a new war and a foreign invasion inflicted on his English subjects were, in the eyes of the army and a minority of MPs, final proof that he could not be trusted. Therefore they argued that it was pointless to negotiate any agreement with him, since he could not be relied upon to maintain it. More importantly, however, they claimed that he had not only forfeited the right to be trusted, he had also forfeited his right to be regarded as God's anointed - by rejecting God's verdict, revealed in his first defeat at parliament's hands, he had rejected God himself, destroyed his own divine status, and should be brought to account for his crimes like any ordinary man.

It is only if the impact of the Second Civil War is seen in relation to the widespread belief in God's Providence that its full significance can be understood. This belief that God directed human behaviour according to his Will and intention was by no means confined to religious radicals, although it was particularly intense among those with strong puritan views. Men who wanted to dedicate their lives to God's service needed to know what God wanted them to do. Their method was to observe the pattern of events and try to work out how God was directing them, seeking in this an understanding of God's purpose and their own place in it. Once God's will was known, their duty was to pursue that purpose with all their strength. It was no coincidence that the army's declaration that Charles I had become a 'man of blood', to be brought to account for his crimes, had come after a long prayer-meeting held at Windsor in April 1648. In this process they had sought to know the Will of God, and having apparently discovered it, to follow its direction.

This pattern of behaviour can be seen again and again in the life of Oliver Cromwell. Before any momentous decision, Cromwell was paralysed by inactivity, until a sign of some kind showed him which way God wished him to go. This was the case in June 1647, when his indecision over the army mutinies was brought to an end by the visit of Cornet Joyce, after which he pursued the army's cause with vigour and determination. At such times, considerations of legality, of conventional loyalties and duties, weighed little in the balance against duty to God. Thus he could justify resisting the legal authority of parliament and coercing the king. The essential importance of the Second Civil War to men like Cromwell therefore went beyond the issue of whether or not Charles could be trusted - by leading the king to renew the struggle and publicly fly in the face of God's verdict, God had placed Charles in conflict with his Will and made it the duty of his servants to bring the king to justice. By comparison, ordinary considerations of legality and respect for authority and kingship were of little importance.

This does not mean that the interpretation of God's will was easy. Cromwell himself agonised over the steps to be taken after the king's second defeat, as his letters of the autumn of 1648 reveal. It has been suggested that he lingered in Yorkshire on military business, while the campaign to bring Charles to justice was led by Ireton, precisely because of his uncertainty. In correspondence with his cousin, Robert Hammond, who was effectively the king's gaoler on the Isle of Wight, Cromwell debated the issue:

1 Dear Robin ... If thou wilt seek, seek to know the mind of God in all that chain of providence, whereby God brought thee thither, and that person [Charles I] to thee; how, before and since, God has ordered him, and affairs concerning him: and then tell me whether
5 there be not some glorious and high meaning in all this ...
  You say: God hath appointed authorities among the nations, to which active or passive obedience is to be yielded. This resides in England in the parliament ... To this I ... desire thee to see what thou findest in thy own heart as to two or three plain
10 considerations. First, whether *Salus Populi* [the safety of the people] be a sound position? Secondly, whether in the way in hand [parliament's new negotiations with the king] this be provided for, or the whole fruit of the war like to be frustrated, and all most like to turn to what it was or worse? Thirdly, whether this army be not a
15 lawful power, called by God to oppose and fight against the king upon such stated grounds ...?
  But truly these kinds of reasonings may be but fleshly, either with or against: only it is good to try what truth may be in them. And the Lord teach us. My dear friend, let us look into
20 providences; surely they mean somewhat. They hang so together; have been so constant, so clear and unclouded ...

What is clear from these letters is that Cromwell was not unaware of the logical arguments for and against a settlement with the king, nor of the dangers inherent in either path - but what is crucial is that, if convinced that either policy was God's will, he would have little hesitation in pursuing it. Hence the essential significance of the Second Civil War was to convince some that Charles must be brought to justice because his crimes and his untrustworthiness merited it, and to convince others that this must be done because it was the will of God and their overriding duty. While both motives were important (and not always distinguishable or separable) it was the latter which gave social conservatives like Cromwell the stomach for revolution.

While Cromwell debated in the North, the army's attack on the king was orchestrated by Henry Ireton. His task was made easier by the king, who dragged out negotiations with parliament's commissioners and privately informed his friends that he would not regard himself as bound by any 'mock-treaty'. In the meantime Ireton persuaded a reluctant Fairfax that the army should have its say, and entered new discussions with the Levellers - this time, however, the army was represented entirely by its officers. While these discussions continued, he compiled a new *Remonstrance* which was presented to parliament as the view of the army on 20 November. Its text is interesting, in that it combined both human and providential arguments against the king:

> 1 Where a person trusted with a limited power to rule according to laws and ... with express covenant and oath also [the king's coronation oath] obliged to preserve and protect the rights and liberties of the people, for, and by whom he is entrusted shall not
> 5 only pervert that trust and abuse that power ... but also ... rise to the assuming of hurtful powers which he never had committed to him, and indeed take away all those foundations of right and liberty, and of redress or remedy too ... and shall fly to the way of force upon his trusting people and attempt by it to uphold and
> 10 establish himself in that absolute tyrannical power ... such a person, in so doing, does forfeit all that trust and power he had; and absolving the people from the bonds of covenant and peace betwixt him and them, does set them free to take their best advantage, and, if he fall within their power, to to proceed in
> 15 judgement against him, even for that alone, if there were no more.

However, the *Remonstrance* continued, there was much more to be brought against Charles. As Derek Hirst summarised, 'the king had repeatedly broken his contract with [the people], and God had repeatedly witnessed against him'. While the document called for him to be brought to justice, it did not, however, argue for the complete abolition of monarchy. That act would be justified later in works such as John Milton's *Tenure of Kings and Magistrates* (1649) after the step had already been taken. Derek Hirst has suggested that this caution was dictated by Cromwell's reluctance to consider such a step, but it may have been Ireton's own preference for keeping possible options open. The need to remove Charles was clear; how to replace him was another matter.

The army was given little opportunity to debate this matter. While its remonstrances were ignored, the parliamentary majority pushed ahead with the proposed treaty with the king. In early December the commissioners returned from the Isle of Wight with the king's answer to four bills, and although he had rejected parliament's proposals regarding the Church, the conservatives were heartened by his concessions over the militia. On 5 December the House of Commons voted that his answers were sufficient basis for further negotiations. This was undoubtedly a prelude to his return to London and a rapid settlement. Seeing their concerns and interests ignored and about to be sacrificed, the army acted. Ireton wished to dissolve the House of Commons and hold new elections on a reformed franchise. He was dissuaded from this by the radical MPs, such as the republicans Thomas Scot and Edmund Ludlow, who had now aligned themselves with the army. They argued that a military intervention would be unpopular and that elections would probably go against them. It was decided, therefore, to purge the present parliament, and leave the settlement in the hands of the minority who would be left.

The participation of a minority of MPs in this process, and the determination of others to settle with the king despite his untrustworthiness and minimal concessions, raises some interesting questions about the different parliamentary factions and their motivations. Attempts to label groups of MPs as Presbyterians and Independents, or radicals and republicans, tend to disguise as much as they reveal, and we cannot simply assume that all MPs who acted in a particular way did so for the same reasons. Nevertheless, there were deep and serious divisions among MPs about how to proceed, and the army certainly thought they could tell their friends from their enemies when they forcibly excluded the latter from parliament. An interesting and impressive attempt to study the views and motivations of different MPs was carried out by David Underdown in his *Pride's Purge*, published in 1971. Using the votes registered by MPs themselves and the lists of members excluded by the army, Underdown divided the Commons into five groups on the basis of how they acted and reacted to the trial and execution of the king. These were:

> 71 Revolutionaries, who actively supported the trial and execution;
> 83 Conformists, who accepted the event and participated in parliament thereafter;
> 86 Abstainers, who were not excluded by the army, but who chose to stay away from parliament in order to dissociate themselves from the action against the king;
> 186 Secluded MPs who were excluded from parliament by the army because they had supported the treaty with the king; and
> 45 imprisoned MPs, who were imprisoned by the army because they were seen as the strongest supporters of the agreement with the king.

Underdown then investigated the lives, circumstances and attitudes of these MPs, in order to evaluate the characteristics and motives that led them to act as they did. His conclusions reinforce Derek Hirst's arguments regarding the fluidity of parliamentary factions and the complex considerations that led MPs to act in a particular way. Party labels are rarely relevant, and are often confusing. More recently, however, Underdown's figures have been used as the basis of statistical analysis on computer, and while this also supports the argument that MPs could not be divided into clear-cut parties, it has produced some broad conclusions that may indicate something of MPs' motives and considerations. In many cases the evidence is limited and fragmented, and there are many MPs whose attitudes simply remain unknown.

However, in comparing particular characteristics across the five groups of MPs, two interesting points stand out. In general terms, the Secluded and Imprisoned MPs who supported the treaty with the king were of higher social status and income than those who supported the king's execution. This might help to explain their determination to defend both the existing political system and the structure of society by retaining a powerful monarchy and a state church. But it would be dangerous to pursue this line too far for the difference is not great - all MPs were members of the governing classes, and there were a significant number of the most wealthy and important members who associated themselves with the 'revolution' in some way. The second point is more clear-cut. Among the Revolutionaries and Conformists who supported or acquiesced in the trial and execution, a large number are known to have held strong, and often radical religious views.

Again, however, the generalisation should not be taken too far. The religious views of many MPs are unrecorded, and not all revolutionaries can be shown to have been influenced by religion. Nevertheless, individual case studies have shown that many of the wealthiest and most important supporters of the revolution had strong religious views. Therefore, it seems that it can be said with confidence that this evidence enhances the importance of the religious issues and attitudes that have been put forward above as significant factors in bringing about the execution of the king. It could further be suggested that wealth and social status had a negative importance, tending to incline MPs against radical solutions and in favour of defending the existing system, while religious commitment exercised a positive effect, causing some MPs to act in a revolutionry, or radical way even against their own material interests. What is clearest of all is that, in describing how MPs divided over the issue of settlement, we are not looking at coherent parties or even factions, but at men who shared many of the same beliefs and concerns and who made individual decisions in the light of a number of, often conflicting, influences and considerations.

Few men demonstrate these complex and conflicting motivations more clearly than the supposed 'arch-revolutionary', Oliver Cromwell. The tone of his letter to Robert Hammond (quoted on page 130) and his delay in returning to London are indications of his uncertainty and the conflicting considerations that influenced his decisions. On 6 December the parliament buildings were surrounded by troops from the regiment of Colonel Pride. Conservative MPs were excluded, and others, hearing of what was happening, chose to stay away. The most prominent supporters of the proposed treaty were imprisoned, although Denzil Holles had been warned and had already left the country. Initially, those who chose to enter the Commons had difficulty in establishing a quorum of forty, but in the following weeks more MPs returned, partly as a result of persuasion by Cromwell. He had reached London on 7 December and declared his support for the purge. However it was by no means certain that he had yet decided in favour of bringing the king to trial, and he continued to counsel caution until the end of the month. Nor was he alone in this. It is often assumed that Pride's Purge was a deliberate step towards the king's trial and execution, but it is worth remembering that the timing had been dictated by parliament rather than the army, and that the purge was in some ways a defensive step, intended to prevent the majority in parliament from, as the army saw it, betraying themselves and their cause.

However, if the die was not cast at the time of the purge, the remaining days of December completed the process. Cromwell still hesitated, and seems to have attempted to persuade Charles to make some meaningful concessions, but the king refused. This may well have been interpreted by Cromwell as the sign from God that he had been waiting for; thereafter he seems to have pushed forward the trial and its inevitable conclusion with all speed. He was determined that, if Charles was to be removed, it would be by public trial, with charges openly brought and justified. If such a trial were to take place, however, there could be no doubt of its outcome. Acquittal would leave the problems of settlement even less capable of solution. Once found guilty, Charles would have to be executed. It was clear that he would never agree to abdicate, imprisonment would leave him free to plot and foment further rebellions, and overseas exile would simply invite him to raise a new army and return.

That still did not mean that the abolition of the monarchy had to follow. A minority of MPs had now committed themselves to republicanism, but many of those who were not prepared to see the return of Charles Stuart had no such commitment, and the views of the army officers seemed mixed. According to Bulstrode Whitelocke, one of the Rump (the name given to the MPs who remained in parliament after Pride's Purge) on 23 December a meeting of MPs discussed various means of replacing Charles.

1 Sir Thomas Widdrington and I went together, according to appointment to the Speaker's house. There we met various gentlemen of the House, and we consulted about settling the kingdom by the parliament, and not to leave all to the sword ...
5 Some of them were wholly against any king at all; others were

against having the present king, or his eldest son or his second son to be king; others were for the third son, the Duke of Gloucester (who was among them and might be educated as they should appoint) to be made king. They came, after a long debate, to no
10 resolution at all.

Cromwell and some officers had similar views to these MPs, but many of the officers favoured a republican solution. Nevertheless, it was two months after the king's execution that the step was finally taken to end the monarchy and establish the republican Commonwealth. It is difficult to escape the conclusion that the overriding reason for the abolition of the monarchy was the lack of a viable replacement for Charles. There was simply no acceptable or safe candidate for the throne.

On 1 January 1649 the Rump agreed to establish a High Court to try the king; the remaining Lords objected, but the Rump simply declared the Commons able to make law without them. The king's trial opened on 20 January, with John Bradshaw as Lord President of the Court. Charles was brought in, and the charge read; he had tried, it was claimed 'to erect and uphold in himself an unlimited and tyrannical power to rule according to his will and to overthrow the rights and liberties of the people'. He had waged war on the parliament, granted commissions to Irish rebels, and was thus responsible for all the death, damage and destruction thereby created. Charles responded with dignity. Claiming to have received his trust from God, he denied that the court had any right to try him, and refused to plead. With strength and courage he declared that 'I do stand more for the liberty of my people than any here that come to be my pretended judges. And therefore let me know by what lawful authority I am seated here, and I will answer it. Otherwise I will not answer it.' When the verdict was returned and sentenced pronounced, he tried to speak, but was denied the right. 'I am not suffered to speak', he declared 'expect what justice other people will have'. When the sentence was carried out on 30 January, eyewitnesses described the 'mighty groan' that came from the people present.

There is little doubt that Charles served the cause of monarchy better by his death than ever he had in his life. The publication and massive sales of *Eikon Basilike,* supposedly the dead king's memoirs written during his last days, fed the myth of martyrdom, but Charles himself had laid the groundwork by his courage and dignity in death, and by the force of his argument. However justified Cromwell and his allies might feel in the eyes of God, they had behaved illegally in the eyes of the law, and continued to do so. This was to be the fatal flaw and weakness that undermined all their efforts to achieve a stable regime thereafter, and led ultimately to the restoration of the monarchy in 1660. Yet for all his admirable qualities in these last days, a dispassionate examination of what brought Charles to that position must surely find that, for whatever

The Execution of Charles I

reason or principle, he himself had been the greatest single cause of his own trial and execution.

2 Making Notes: Why was Charles I Executed in 1649?

Before investigating the causes of the king's execution in 1649, you will find it useful to consolidate your understanding of the material contained in this chapter by making notes on the events of 1648-9 and analysing the attitudes and ideas that influenced their outcome. Use the following headings to organise your notes:

The Execution of the King.
1. The Second Civil War
   (a) military significance
   (b) political effects - distrust of the king
                        - ideas/attitudes, belief in Providence
2. Trial and Execution
   (a) attempts at settlement
   (b) Pride's Purge
   (c) attitudes and motives
   (d) the king's death

Given their importance in the final outcome, it would be useful to explore more fully the beliefs and attitudes of those who supported the king's execution. You would therefore find it helpful to answer the following source-based questions before proceeding further.

Source-based questions on 'The Execution of Charles I'

1 The Role of Providence.
Re-read Cromwell's letter to Robert Hammond, printed on page 130 and answer the following questions.
(a) What events might Cromwell consider to be the "chain of providence" that had brought Charles into Hammond's care? (4 marks)
(b) Who does he believe to be in control of those events? (1 mark)
(c) What "glorious and high meaning" could these events imply? (3 marks)
(d) What does Cromwell mean by the term "Salus Populi" and whether it "be provided for" in parliament's negotiations? (3 marks)
(e) On what basis could the army be considered "a lawful power"? (3 marks)
(f) Cromwell later dismisses these considerations as "fleshly reasonings" What does he mean by this? (3 marks)

(g) What does Cromwell expect Hammond to do when he advises him to "look into providences? (3 marks)

(h) In the light of these statements, explain Cromwell's belief in Providence and how it might influence his actions. (5 marks)

Now re-read the Army's Remonstrance, written by Ireton. (page 131)

(i) What arguments does Ireton use to justify the king's trial? (3 marks)

(j) In what ways do these arguments differ from those put forward by Cromwell? Do they conflict? (4 marks)

(k) Why might these two documents emphasise different aspects of the beliefs that justified the king's execution? (4 marks)

(l) Using all the information that you have gathered, explain why some officers and MPs believed that the king should be brought to trial in 1648-9. (14 marks)

The final section of this chapter is intended to address a major issue of the period, and to offer an example of essay writing based on the methodological approach that has been followed in the study guides to the preceding chapters. The approach is indicated by brief section headings, and it is intended that, as you read the essay, you should be able to compile a list of causal factors to provide you with a basis for planning and writing responses to a range of different essay questions on this topic. As a final exercise you should then try to devise different possible questions and discuss them before choosing one to write.

Conclusion: 'Why was Charles I executed in 1649?'

1 Introduction
(Use to analyse the question and establish issues to be addressed.)

The execution of Charles I was an event without parallel in Europe before the French Revolution of 1789. It was not unknown for inadequate monarchs to be deposed, and even murdered, but to bring an anointed monarch to public trial, to condemn him to death and to justify this in the name of the people was unprecedented. The event requires explanation because it was revolutionary and because it was not the expected or intended result of the Civil War. In turn, this suggests two possible explanations as to why it occurred. It can be argued that an event of such significance can only be explained by long-term changes in the nature of society, its beliefs and attitudes; alternatively, the continuing search for a settlement after 1646 could indicate that the trial and execution of the king was the unexpected and unintended result of errors and misjudgements in the crucial years of 1646-9.

2 The Conditional Factors

An examination of English society in the century before the Civil War does reveal a number of significant changes and developments. The Reformation had established religious doctrines which emphasised the importance of individual faith and individual interpretation. The immediate effect was to create conflict within the Church and within society, and to make the monarch directly responsible for these divisive issues. The long-term result was to undermine authority in religion and encourage separatism and claims to individual rights. In addition, the development of the concept of King-in-parliament as the supreme power in the state increased the status and significance of parliament at a time when social and economic changes (to which the Reformation also contributed) were increasing the numbers and wealth of the gentry who dominated the House of Commons. Protestant reforms ended the clerical monopoly of education and produced a more educated and articulate laity; and at the higher social levels these qualities were encouraged by the growing reliance upon the gentry in government and administration. Combined with the financial problems of the monarchy, these conditions created tensions and stresses within the structure of government, which, if badly handled, could develop into open conflict.

Yet there is little evidence in the events leading up to war in 1642 of any desire to radically change the system of government, let alone remove the monarch as the centre of power. Those who led the struggle against Charles I were seeking to resist infringements of their rights and privileges, and to secure a reformed Protestant Church. What was radical in their behaviour was their willingness to change the balance of the constitution in order to achieve these objectives. It is therefore difficult to argue that long-term changes in social structure, political practice or even political thinking played any significant part in bringing about the revolutionary act of executing Charles I, except in so far as they helped to bring about the Civil War that was its essential pre-condition.

It was, in fact, the war itself that did most to create the potential for revolution. Faced with the need to justify military action, parliament's apologists evolved far more radical political theories than they had previously put forward, in claiming the right to rebel against a monarch who abused his powers. To justify their role, they claimed that parliament represented the people, for whose safety and well-being government was created. In 1646 these arguments were extended by the Levellers into a doctrine of the sovereignty of the people, and in 1649 they formed the basis of the charge of treason upon which the king was tried and condemned. In the same year John Milton's *Tenure of Kings and Magistrates* fashioned these ideas into a republican theory by which to justify the removal of the king and the abolition of the monarchy. In the conditions of war, theory tended to follow practice, and each step moved in a more radical direction.

This was partly the result of the war's impact in other areas, especially its effect on religious ideas and practice. The crisis between king and parliament that developed in 1641 revealed the existence of religious radicals whose separatist organisation, lay preaching and demands for some form of religious toleration undermined authority in church and state. It is clear from their rapid emergence in 1641-2 that these groups were in existence before 1640, and that they originated in the Protestant insistence on an individual, Bible-based faith, but they had remained few and scattered. With the collapse of censorship in 1641 they were able to declare their existence and publish their ideas. Open debate allowed their ideas to develop, and wartime conditions gave them credibility. The conflict between king and parliament reinforced millenarian ideas of a struggle between good and evil which was reaching its climax in England. In these circumstances, separatist congregations increased and a demand for some measure of religious toleration was formulated. The need to campaign for such rights led to demands for freedom of speech and of the press. Political conflict, economic dislocation, religious enthusiasm and militant individualism gave rise to a range of radical ideas, culminating in the democratic republicanism of the Levellers. Perhaps most significant of all, in the New Model Army and its leaders radicals found sympathy and protection. By 1646 the needs and conditions of war had released, if not created, genuinely revolutionary forces within English society.

These developments did not, however, make the king's execution inevitable, or even likely at this stage. Radical ideas were held only by a tiny minority, and the separatists included many members like Cromwell and Ireton, whose political and social attitudes were largely orthodox. When Charles surrendered in 1646, it was assumed that he would bow to the logic of defeat, and accept a negotiated settlement. This was certainly the aim of both parliament and the army leaders in 1646 and throughout 1647. It is therefore necessary to consider what factors prevented this settlement from being achieved, and why some of those involved came to believe that a settlement without the king offered a better alternative.

The most obvious reason for the failure to find a settlement after the first Civil War is the king's refusal to accept any of the propositions put to him. In 1646-7 he rejected the Newcastle Propositions offered by parliament and later the Heads of the Proposals offered by the army. His reluctance to come to terms arose partly from his convictions regarding kingship and his role and power in Church and State. For Charles, kingship was a divinely appointed trust, and to accept any significant reduction of his role would be a failure to do his duty. Similarly, he regarded his right to govern the Church through the ancient institution of bishops as both a social and religious obligation. These matters were not, in fact, negotiable.

In this context, Charles was prepared to delay, prevaricate, or to make short-term concessions, but genuine agreement was not his intention. He was further encouraged in this strategy by the obvious divisions among his enemies. In 1646 there were fears among the English parliamentary leaders that Charles would come to an agreement with their Scottish allies, based upon the imposition of a Presbyterian church system in England in return for the re-establishment of his legal and constitutional powers. By the end of the year this danger had faded, but had been replaced by growing concern at the activities of the radical minority and, in particular, their influence within the parliamentary army. The determination of Holles and the Derby House Committee to remove the radical threat, by disbanding the army, backfired and by May/June 1647 the army was in open revolt. Most crucially of all, the leading officers like Cromwell (and to a lesser extent, Fairfax) had placed army unity above their loyalty to parliament, effectively creating a third political force to complicate the process of settlement.

The politicisation of the army was thus brought about by conservative errors, but its effect was to give a new influence to the radical forces released by the war. In many ways, events had conspired to gather these forces around the army. Its rapid success against the royalist forces had encouraged the belief that such victories were the work of Providence, and that the army was the instrument of God's will. The conservative attack on the army in 1647 had forged a new religious and political unity within its ranks. While the army was not politically representative in any legal or constitutional sense, it did speak on behalf of a section of the population and, in its own eyes, represented God's people and His cause. Hence it was justified in intervening in the process of settlement to protect interests which would otherwise be overlooked and ignored. Its purpose at this stage was to influence the nature of an agreement with the king, not to depose him. In different circumstances, however, it might be capable of contemplating radical solutions if those interests were at risk.

In the short term, these events seemed to work to the advantage of the king, and Charles was not slow to seize his opportunities. Throughout 1647 he played off the army and parliament against each other, and when this failed to produce satisfactory terms, he was able to exploit Scottish fears to renew the war. In December 1647 the Scots signed an Engagement by which they would invade England to restore the king in return for a (temporary) Presbyterian settlement of the Church. Motivated by religious zeal and dislike of radicalism, they were no longer content to leave the matter of settlement to the English. In the face of this military threat, parliament and army were able to set aside their differences, and this second Civil War had little military importance. However, its political significance was immense. Royalist risings in England revealed the extent of popular support for a settlement with the king, strengthening conservative desires for a rapid return to traditional government. At the same time, the war convinced the army and its supporters that a settlement with the king was impossible and created, for the first time, a real possibility that they would seek a settlement without him.

By the autumn of 1648, therefore, parliament's supporters were more deeply divided than ever. Fear of radicalism and the threat represented by radical groups, as well as resentment of the army's interference in political matters, was deep-rooted among the majority of MPs and the governing class that they represented. Although the parliamentary majority voted in January 1648 against further negotiations with the king who had so clearly betrayed their trust, they were in fact incapable of visualising any other solution. Belief in a social hierarchy which was defended and maintained by monarchy, and fears of social disintegration if the controlling influence of Church and king was weakened meant that, ultimately, they depended on the king's co-operation in any settlement. When Charles told the parliamentary commissioners in 1647 that 'without me you will fall', he was stating what they believed, as well as his own convictions. When the Second Civil War ended in the early autumn of 1648, the parliamentary majority saw no option other than the renewal of negotiations, even at the cost of significant concessions to the king.

The army and its supporters disagreed. Charles's cynical betrayal of those who sought to negotiate with him had finally convinced many of them that no settlement could be secure because Charles could not be trusted to maintain it. His willingness to break promises which he regarded as extorted from him could be traced back to the Petition of Right in 1628, and his behaviour in the long term must be seen as a significant factor in the distrust that had now reached new heights. In this context, the Second Civil War provided final and undeniable proof that Charles was unfit to govern. An army Remonstrance, written by Henry Ireton and presented to parliament on 20 November declared that he had betrayed his trust and that parliament had a right and duty, as the nation's representative, to depose him for the nation's safety. These views were supported by a minority of republican MPs, such as Sir Arthur Haselrig and Henry Marten. Drawing on classical examples and parliament's own justification for taking up arms, they justified the king's trial in political terms, and saw the Second Civil War as proof of his betrayal.

For others, particularly the army leaders, the influence of religion was more important. Desire for a measure of toleration 'for tender consciences' to meet outside the confines of the national Church was a consideration, but more influential in this context was the widespread and intense belief in the role of God's providence in human affairs. For most puritans, particularly of the more radical kind, events were to be seen and interpreted as evidence of God's will. Thus the victory of parliament in 1646 was interpreted as God's verdict on the struggle, and the instrument of victory, the New Model Army as having been called by God to defend his cause. When Charles renewed the war in 1648, he was not merely betraying his trust, he was rejecting the will of God and thereby forfeiting the divine status accorded to a Christian monarch. When God made him behave in this way it could only signify that God had abandoned him - it was therefore the duty of those who wished to serve God to bring the man, Charles Stuart, to justice.

By December 1648, therefore, a combination of conditional factors had made the trial and execution of Charles I likely, but not yet certain. The impact of the war on extreme Protestant beliefs had created radical forces, capable of radical solutions. These could have been contained if king and parliament had been able to conclude an agreement in 1646-7, but Charles's character and beliefs made this impossible. The Second Civil War, initiated by the king, had convinced these radical forces that he ought to be brought to justice, because there was no alternative and because it was the will of God. At this point, however, the outcome was still uncertain and the means of attaining it even more so. In the first place the radicals did not, apparently, have the full support of Cromwell, who seems to have deliberately remained in Yorkshire on military duties. Secondly, the army petitions seem to have been intended to persuade rather than coerce the parliamentary majority, and it is unlikely that they would ever have succeeded. It was clearly within the power of the army leaders to impose a settlement of their choice, but the ability to impose a settlement did not necessarily provide the will to do so. The army leaders hesitated to take such a revolutionary step, and it was the actions of the conservatives in parliament, and of the king himself, that finally brought it about.

3 The Contingent Factors

What sparked off the final crisis was the determination of parliamentary conservatives to conclude an agreement with the king that would enable them to destroy the radical threat. On 5 December they voted the king's replies to their latest offers to be a suitable basis for negotiation. The threat of a conservative settlement, betraying all that they had fought for, forced the army to act on 6 December and to purge parliament. Pride's Purge, retrospectively approved by Cromwell, was the beginning of the process by which Charles was brought to trial, but its timing was dictated by conservative initiatives rather than the army. Even then, Cromwell seems to have tried to find a compromise solution, to persuade Charles to make some concession. The king's refusal seems to have finally convinced Cromwell that trial and execution were the will of God, after which he supported the process with energy and determination. Once the trial began, there could be no doubt about the verdict and sentence. To acquit Charles was unthinkable, and to leave him alive, in prison or in exile, would simply enable him to initiate new wars and invasions. If Charles could not return to his throne on terms which ensured the security of the opposition and their cause, his trial and execution were the only other viable option.

4 Conclusion - the Relative Importance of Different Factors

It is clear that many different factors played a part in bringing about the execution of Charles I in 1649, with varying degrees of significance. One way of evaluating the significance of these factors is to consider how the necessary combination built up, to the point where the execution of the king became the most likely outcome of the situation. Religious and political conflict, and the character and beliefs of the king were present at the end of the First Civil War in 1646, yet there was no suggestion that the king should be brought to trial, let alone deposed and executed. Hence, although these factors created the pre-conditions that allowed the king's execution, they cannot be sufficient in themselves to explain it. The death of Charles was not the inevitable result of underlying social, religious or political changes. By the autumn of 1648, however, a large section of the army and some MPs had become convinced that the king could, and should, be brought to account. Moreover, when the parliamentary majority ignored their views, they felt justified in overriding the law, the rights of parliament and popular opinion in order to impose them. It required provocation by parliamentary conservatives to finally force them into action, but given the attitudes of conservative MPs and the king's aims, this was almost bound to happen. Hence the key factors lie in three developments which occurred between the end of 1646 and the autumn of 1648. The first was the emergence of radicalism and the politicisation of the army, creating a political force which was capable of revolutionary action. The second was the king's continuing refusal to come to a workable settlement, removing all viable alternatives. The third was the Second Civil War and Charles's responsibility for it, which both demonstrated the need for a radical solution and provided the its justification. It can thus be said that it was the interaction of these factors, in the context of changing attitudes produced by war and upheaval, that brought about the king's execution.

It is true, therefore, that the public trial and execution of Charles I cannot be explained without reference to long term political, social and religious developments, not because these were necessarily revolutionary but because they created the conditions of war and upheaval in which revolutionary forces could take shape. Yet it was the errors and miscalculations of Charles and his parliamentary opponents that enabled, or drove, this revolutionary minority to take action. Their refusal to accommodate the interests of the radical minority, particularly in religion, created a new political force around the army. The king's continued and stubborn rejection of God's will and cause left no room for compromise. In 1642 his intransigence led to war, in 1646 to stalemate; in the changed conditions of 1649, it led to his own downfall, and that of the monarchy itself.

Answering essay questions on 'The Execution of Charles I'

Drawing on your notes and the list of causal factors that you have compiled from the account above, plan possible answers to the essay questions set out below. You should then choose one essay to write.

1. 'The most important cause of the execution of Charles I was Charles himself.' How far do you agree?
2. How far can the execution of Charles I be explained by reference to the actions of the army and its supporters?
3. 'Although it could not be foreseen at the time, the execution of Charles I was inevitable from the time of his defeat in 1646.' Do you agree?
4. How far can the execution of Charles I be described as a revolutionary act?
5. 'The execution of Charles I cannot be understood without studying the religious outlook of his contemporaries.' How far would you agree?

CHAPTER 8

Conclusion: a British Revolution?

In the Introduction to this book a number of issues were raised which have been, and are, the subject of debate among historians. Of these, two in particular require judgements to be made by considering the events of the period as a whole. The first is the argument, put forward by Conrad Russell and supported by John Morrill, that the English Civil War cannot be viewed in isolation from events elsewhere in Britain. The second is the question of whether the Civil Wars can be considered to have constituted a 'revolution'. This Conclusion therefore attempts to do two things. The first is to explore the issue of a British dimension, and to extend it to offer one interpretation of the nature and impact of the civil wars. The second is to suggest some approaches to the idea of revolution, including that of a British Revolution, and to encourage you to consider, debate and defend your own judgements on the matter.

In Russell's view the English Civil Wars should more properly be considered the British Civil Wars of 1637-1651, beginning with the outbreak of violent resistance to the Prayer Book in Scotland. He argues that the difficulties of ruling three kingdoms, each with its own legal and religious systems, covering four different cultural units, were a major cause of the breakdown that occurred in the mid-seventeenth century. He also suggests that this breakdown did not occur first in England (indeed he suggests that it would have been unlikely to occur at all if left to the English) but in the peripheral kingdoms which were further from the centre of control, and that thereafter the upheavals in England were in many ways a reaction to events elsewhere. At the very least, he contends, events in England were affected at crucial times by the actions and interventions of the Scots and Irish. John Morrill has suggested that, if anything, Russell's analysis does not go far enough, and that historians of the Civil War should be seeking to study the development of Britain as a whole, and the causes and significance of the mid-seventeenth century crisis within this context.

It is clear from the previous chapters that this argument is largely proven. The religious crisis provoked by Charles divided both English and Scots, and the resulting factions and alliances transcended geographical boundaries. The Civil Wars began with the Scottish rebellion of 1637-40 (the Bishops' Wars) and the parliamentary opposition in England were politically allied with the Scottish Covenanters long before they concluded a military alliance in 1643. Whether or not Russell is correct in identifying anti-Scottish feeling as a factor in the emergence of a moderate royalist group in England, it is clear that dislike of Scottish Presbyterianism was a significant and continuing factor among English parliamentarians throughout the period. Whether or not the Scots had an 'imperial vision', as he suggests, they certainly had a religious vision, and their pursuit of this goal led them to influence English affairs in 1640, in 1643-6, and again in 1648 on behalf of the king. A similar case can be made for Ireland. The Stuart policy of Protestant 'plantation' had created a religious division in Ireland, whose violent eruption in 1641 was crucial in bringing the parliamentary conflict in England to the point of war. The continuing claim that the king was in contact with Irish rebels was one of parliament's strongest propaganda points throughout the period, and was specifically referred to at his trial. It is clear that the British kingdoms were torn apart by religious division, and that in the mid-seventeenth century, that religious crisis combined with other problems to erupt into Civil War throughout the British Isles.

The point can be further developed by considering what happened when that Civil War ended. From 1646, fighting in England ceased, and was replaced by the search for a settlement. Yet that settlement cannot be considered an English matter, for, as events proved, it was neither final nor secure until accepted by the Scots, Welsh and Irish as well. In 1648 Charles called on his Celtic subjects for aid against the English parliament, and they responded positively. Only by defeating the Scots and Welsh in 1648 could the English parliament impose its wishes on the king, and when the army and parliamentary Rump chose to execute that king, the new order had to be imposed by Cromwell and the army on Ireland in 1649, and on Scotland from 1649 to 1651. What the Civil Wars revealed and reinforced was the fact that matters of government were now British matters - whatever system was established in London had to be accepted throughout Britain in order to survive, and this was now a permanent condition. In 1660, monarchy was restored throughout Britain, and when conflict arose again with James II in 1688, that 'Glorious Revolution' was also enforced throughout Britain as a whole. When Jacobites threatened in Scotland and in Ireland, the English and their Protestant allies in those kingdoms drew more closely together for their mutual benefit to create, over the following century, a United Kingdom.

In one sense, therefore, the term 'British Revolution' may indeed be appropriate. There are many ways of defining the idea of a revolution, one of the most obvious being that it is a violent upheaval which brings about permanent change. Certainly the Civil Wars throughout Britain were violent. It is also the case that they initiated some permanent and important political changes. When the three kingdoms of England, Scotland and Ireland came under the control of one monarch in 1603, they ceased to be viable as separate entities - and if they were to be united, one cultural tradition would inevitably come to dominate. The problem of 'multiple kingdoms' to which Russell refers arose from the natural desire of the monarch to establish uniform systems on his different kingdoms. The main error of Charles I was that he sought to impose this uniformity in the most intensely divisive aspect of government, religion. This led to the rejection of his authority, not in one kingdom, but in all three. However, when the king was defeated, those who sought to replace his authority found it necessary to impose their own in his place. This in turn led to a new power struggle, from which the English parliament emerged victorious. In 1649-51 Cromwell and the army effectively achieved what many monarchs had failed to do - they conquered Scotland and Ireland and secured the permanent dominance of England within the British Isles.

This development cannot be attributed to the Civil Wars alone. It arose from the dynastic ambitions shared by most monarchs, and from the superior wealth and power enjoyed by England as the largest and most fertile of the British kingdoms. Nevertheless, the Civil Wars were a turning point in three crucial ways. They demonstrated more clearly than ever before that the three kingdoms could not develop in isolation, and demonstrated to the English governing class their need to dominate. Secondly, they provided the occasion for that dominance to be secured militarily, and thirdly, they permitted the experiment of a united kingdom, foreshadowing the modern arrangement. Hence they could be said to have initiated revolutionary political changes in the government of Britain, and indeed in the concept of Britain itself.

1 A Revolution in Britain?

The argument set out above has offered one definition of 'revolution' - that it is a violent upheaval which causes or initiates permanent and significant change - but this raises as many questions as it answers. For example, 'change' can be of many kinds and affect different areas of life. Are political, economic, social and ideological changes all of equal importance, and equally 'revolutionary'? How long must a change endure to be considered 'permanent'? How great, or long-lasting, do changes have to be in order to be 'significant'? There is, in effect, little value in definitions of this kind except as a starting-point for discussion. An alternative strategy may be to define certain characteristics that are associated with the idea of revolution, and to use these as separate criteria for assessing how far events such as the Civil Wars can be considered revolutionary. These criteria cannot be related only to the effects or results of events - ideas, intentions and motivations can also be of importance. Is it, for example, possible for a revolution to occur without being intended? Are revolutionary intentions or ideas significant even if their effects are temporary or their aims are not fulfilled?

There is, in fact, no final answer to the question of whether or not the Civil Wars constituted a revolution. Not only have historians produced a variety of answers, they have based these on an equal variety of definitions of what a revolution requires. The value of the debate is not in the answers that it draws out, but in the process involved in establishing those anwers. By asking the question, historians are encouraged to analyse the causes, nature and impact of the Civil Wars as well as their long-term effects. By using the study guide set out below, you are now invited to do the same.

___

Study Guide - Was there a mid-seventeenth century revolution?

Consider the comments below, and use them to construct your key criteria for 'revolution'. You may use what is offered, select from it, alter or extend it - these suggestions are intended as a starting point for consideration, not a comprehensive framework. You should then work with a partner or in a group to establish joint criteria, examine the evidence that you have collected from the preceding chapters, and prepare a presentation and defence of your collective view as to whether or not there was a revolution in England (or Britain) in the mid-seventeenth century.

1. Causes - a revolution must arise, at least in part, from some long-term, structural problems. Otherwise it is little more than a coup or a power struggle.
2. Motives - motives need not be consciously revolutionary. However there does need to be some set of beliefs or ideals which the 'revolutionaries' are pursuing or defending. Revolutions are not made by ideologies alone, but it is difficult to conceive of a revolution which is completely without ideology.
3. Events - all the major revolutions (e.g. French or Russian) have been complex sequences of events, developing over a period of time and often in unexpected ways. Most revolutions have seen radical groups and ideas develop after, rather than before, the first upheavals. Some individual events and actions can be revolutionary in themselves.
4. Changes - most revolutions have involved political change, but some would argue that a significant measure of social change or re-organisation is also essential. This might involve changes in the social structure, but it can also relate to the distribution of wealth, the distribution of political power, or even ideas about society and how it should be organised. Changes in attitudes and ideas are often difficult to measure. The most controversial aspects of change are those involving judgements about the extent, significance and permanence of the changes brought about. They are, and will remain, matters of opinion which are valid if there is supporting evidence.
5. Reactions - it is important to remember that historical events occur within particular periods, and their significance needs to be measured in the context of the attitudes and beliefs current at the time. Hence contemporary reactions can be a useful yardstick in judging how revolutionary an event may have been.

Comparative Chart of the Main Peace Terms

	Nineteen Propositions	Oxford Propositions	Uxbridge Propositions	Newcastle Propositions	Heads of the Proposals	Four Bills
Parliaments	Triennial Act stands	Triennial Act stands	Triennial Act stands	Triennial Act stands	Triennial Act repealed; biennial parliaments	Triennial Act stands
Privy Councillors	Parliament to approve					
Officers of State	Parliament to approve 16		Parliament to nominate 13	Parliament to nominate 13	Parliament to nominate for 10 years	
Militia	King to accept Militia Ordinance	King to settle with Parliament's advice	To be settled by Commissioners named by Parliament	Parliament to control for 20 years	Parliament to control for 10 years	Parliament to control for 20 years
Church government	Reformed with Parliament's advice	Bishops etc. abolished	Bishops etc. abolished; reforms advised by Westminster Assembly	Bishops etc. abolished; Presbyterian church for 3 yrs	Bishops etc. cannot coerce; no Presbyterian church	Bishops etc. abolished; Presbyterian church for 3 yrs
Papists	Existing laws to be enforced	Existing laws to be enforced	Existing laws to be enforced	Existing laws to be enforced	Existing laws to be abolished & new ones made	Existing laws to be enforced
Royalists not to be pardoned	—	2	58	58	7	58
Dismissals from office	—	2 for life	48 for life	48 for life	Parliament's enemies for 5 yrs	48 for life

Chronological Table

1625	Accession of Charles I
	Marriage of Charles to Henrietta Maria
1626	William Laud appointed Bishop of London
1627	Five Knights' Case; forced loans declared to be legal
1628	Petition of Right
	Assassination of Buckingham
1628	Sir Thomas Wentworth appointed President of the Council of the North, and a Privy Councillor in 1629
1629	The Three Resolutions and Dissolution of Parliament
1632	Wentworth appointed Lord Deputy of Ireland
1633	Laud became Archbishop of Canterbury
1634	Ship Money levied
1635	Ship Money levied and extended to inland areas
1637	Hampden Case; judges found for the king by 5 to 3
	Charles imposed the use of an adapted Prayer Book in Scotland
1638	The Scots entered a National Covenant for the defence of their religion (Feb.) and abolished Bishops (Nov.)
1639	First Bishops' War, ending in the Treaty of Berwick
1640	Scottish Synod voted to abolish the Prayer Book and Bishops
	Sir Thomas Wentworth created Lord Strafford; became king's chief adviser
	Short Parliament called in England (April); dissolved in May
	Laudian 'Canons' (codifying and enforcing Laudian reforms in the English Church) published in June
	Second Bishops' War (June-Oct.) ending in Treaty of Ripon
	Calling of the Long Parliament (November); impeachment of Laud and Strafford begun
	Petition for abolition of Bishops 'Root and Branch' presented to the House of Commons (December); Laudian Canons declared illegal because they were not confirmed by parliament (16 Dec.) Laud imprisoned in the Tower of London (18 Dec.)
1641 Jan.	Bishops dismissed from political office
Feb.	Triennial Act passed
March	First Army Plot
April	Attainder Act against Strafford introduced
May	Bishops' Exclusion Bill sent to Lords (1 May)
	Army Plot revealed to Commons by Pym (3 May)
	Strafford's Attainder signed by the king (10 May)

	Act against Dissolution of parliament without its consent (10 May)
	May 12, Execution of Strafford
	Root and Branch Bill debated in the Commons; laid aside on May 27
May/June	Second Army plot 1641
June	Lords rejected the Bishops' Exclusion Bill (8 June)
	Ten Propositions presented to the king (24 June)
July	Acts abolishing the Prerogative Courts of Star Chamber and High Commission
Aug.	Ship Money declared illegal
	King left to visit Scotland on 13 Aug.
Sept./Oct.	Parliament not in session
Oct.	23 Oct. Irish rebellion broke out
	30 Oct. Second Army plot revealed
Nov.	Grand Remonstrance passed (22 Nov.)
Dec.	Militia Bill introduced (7 Dec.)
	Grand Remonstrance printed and published (15 Dec.)
1642 Jan.	King's attempt to arrest the five MPs (4 Jan.)
	King left London (10 Jan.)
Feb.	Bishops excluded from the House of Lords
	The queen sailed to seek military help in Holland and France (Feb 13)
Mar.	Militia Ordinance passed by parliament (5 March)
April	King denied entrance to Hull (23 April)
June	The Nineteen Propositions sent from parliament to king
July	Parliament established a Committee of Safety (4 July) and voted to raise an army (12 July)
Aug.	The king raised his standard at Nottingham (22 Aug.)
Oct.	Battle of Edgehill; king able to move towards London
Nov.	Royal forces stopped at Battle of Turnham Green; king retreated to winter in Oxford
1643 May	Peace negotiations at Oxford failed
June	Battle of Adwalton Moor; defeat of parliamentarians in Yorkshire, Fairfax retreated to Hull
	Solemn League and Covenant (alliance) concluded between parliament and Scots
	Assembly of Divines set up to plan reform of the Church
July	Royalists began the Siege of Hull
	Prince Rupert captured Bristol; Charles began the siege of Gloucester (July/Aug)
Sept.	Earl of Essex relieved Gloucester and defeated royalists at Newbury
	Solemn League and Covenant ratified by both Houses
	Charles signed Cessation treaty with Irish rebels

Oct.	Siege of Hull broken; parliamentary control of Lincolnshire and East Yorkshire secured
Dec.	Death of John Pym
1644 Feb.	Independents in the Assembly of Divines published arguments in favour of limited religious toleration; toleration campaign grew throughout the year
July	Parliaméntary victory at Marston Moor
Sept.	Essex trapped in Cornwall; surrendered entire army at Respryn Bridge
Sept./Nov.	Parliamentary crisis; religious and political divisions symbolised by Manchester/Cromwell quarrel.
Dec.	Self-denying Ordinance introduced finally passed in April 1645
1645 Jan./March	Formation of New Model Army
	Growing evidence of Scottish dislike of new developments strained the alliance
	Growing war-weariness in the country; Clubmen risings in the west
	Peace talks entered at Uxbridge; failed because of religious issues and mutual distrust
June	Battle of Naseby; military and political disaster for the king
July	Goring (royalist) defeated at Langport
Sept.	Prince Rupert forced to surrender Bristol; Scottish royalists defeated by the Covenanters
Sept/Oct.	Clubmen risings in Sussex and Wales
1646 April	The king left Oxford and surrendered to the Scots
June	Surrender of Oxford marked the virtual end of the war Leveller demonstrations in London. Thomas Edwards published *Gangraena,* a bitter attack on radicalism
July	Peace terms offered to the king at Newcastle
1647 Feb.	Scots handed king to parliament and left England Parliament voted for disbandment of the Army
April/May	Army petitions and election of Agitators. Regiments refused to disband on May 31
June	Seizure of the king by Cornet Joyce (June 4) Army Engagement - General Council set up (June 5) *Representation of the Army* published
July	Royalist mobs invaded parliament; Independent MPs fled
Aug.	*Heads of the Proposals* presented to the king (Aug.2) Army entered London; conservative leaders fled and the Independents were restored to their seats
Sept.	Army in winter quarters at Putney; Levellers supicious of Grandees' negotiations with the king
Oct.	Leveller John Wildman published the *Case of the Army* Leveller plans, summarised in the *Agreement of the People* debated by the Army Council at Putney

Nov.	The king's escape brought the Putney debates to an end; Leveller mutiny at Ware easily crushed by Cromwell
Dec.	The king signed an *Engagement* inviting the Scots to invade England
1648 Jan.	Parliament voted 'No Further Addresses' to the king Army Council disbanded. Growing discontent and riots in Kent and Essex hardened into royalist risings in April
April	Risings in Kent, Essex, Cornwall, Yorkshire and south Wales; easily dealt with except at Colchester (Essex) and in Wales.
July	Scottish army led by royalist Scots entered England
Aug.	Cromwell completed defeat of Welsh rising and caught the Scots at Preston (17 Aug.) Conservative leaders returned to parliament
Sept.	Colchester forced to surrender to Fairfax. Second Civil War effectively over Parliamentary commissioners sent to the Isle of Wight to renew negotiations with the king
Nov.	Army Remonstrance demanded the trial and punishment of the king
Dec.	House of Commons voted the king's reply to their commissioners to be a basis for negotiation (Dec. 5) Pride's Purge (Dec. 6). Purge approved by Cromwell on his return to London on Dec. 7
1649 Jan.	High Court of Justice set up to try the king (Jan 1) Jan. 20: The king's trial opened Jan. 30: King Charles I was executed at Whitehall Mar. Abolition of the monarchy and House of Lords: England was declared to be a Commonwealth (republic)

Further Reading

An enormous amount has been written about the Civil Wars, much of it still controversial. It is therefore difficult to provide either a bibliography which is in any way exhaustive, or to provide a brief list which does justice to the different arguments and viewpoints. What is offered below is a list of suggestions that students might follow in order to study the period in greater depth, either as a whole or by picking out particular aspects for further investigation. The suggested works include a range of interpretations, so that the different schools of thought are represented. Hence they include some interpretations with which this author is not entirely in agreement - the aim being that students should read, consider and evaluate the different arguments for themselves.

Anyone who wishes to understand the history of the civil wars would find it useful to dip into some of the classic works on the subject, not because the interpretations have gone unchallenged, but because it is these interpretations and the desire to challenge them that have shaped the work of more recent historians. The first general account of the wars, **Clarendon's** *History of the Rebellion* (first published in 1702-4) is still widely available in good libraries, as is **S.R. Gardiner's** *History of England, 1603-56* (1893-6). A very readable biography of Cromwell was produced in 1900 by Gardiner's friend and defender, **C.H. Firth,** while his work on *Cromwell's Army* (1902) provides a useful starting point from which to consider more recent interpretations. Both books were later re-published in paperback. Finally, students who wish to understand why puritanism could be seen, by contemporaries and historians, as a challenging and revolutionary creed, could usefully read the work of **William Haller** in his *Rise of Puritanism* (first published 1938, paperback edition by Harper Torchbooks, 1957) as well as his *Liberty and Reformation in the Puritan Revolution* (New York, 1955).

More recent historiography can be usefully summarised within a number of categories.

General surveys - two very good recent textbooks are **Barry Coward's** *The Stuart Age* (London 1980) and **Roger Lockyer's** *The Early Stuarts* (Longman, 1989). Among older works, **Christopher Hill's** *Century of Revolution* (1961) remains useful. Its approach and interpretation has been challenged, but it remains a mine of information. A clear and accessible account of the period is given in **Derek Hirst,** *Authority and Conflict* (Edward Arnold, 2nd ed. 1987). A number of wider surveys which attempt to set the seventeenth-century crisis in a long-term context are offered by **A.G.R. Smith,** *The Emergence of a Nation State* (Longman 1984), **Conrad Russell,** *The Crisis of Parliaments: English History, 1509-1660* (London 1971), and **R. Ashton,** *Reformation and Revolution, 1558-1660* (London 1984). **Jonathan Clark's** *Revolution* *and Rebellion: State and Society in England in the Seventeenth and Eighteenth Centuries* (Cambridge 1986) has subjected earlier interpretations to severe criticism, but has itself been the subject of critical reviews. The student should judge for him/herself. An interesting fresh interpretation of the period is offered by **J. Goldstone,** *Revolution and Rebellion in the Early Modern World* (University of California 1991), which looks at both the English and French revolutions in the light of demographic changes and their effects on society. While it is not suggested that this is essential reading, it does offer a possible synthesis of many recent conflicting arguments.

The causes and outbreak of the war have been the subject of many conflicting interpretations. A long-term, determinist approach is presented in **Lawrence Stone's** *Causes of the English Revolution* (Routledge 1972) and challenged in the work of Cust and Hughes, Ashton and Fletcher. Of particular value are **R. Ashton,** *The English Civil War, 1603-1649* (1978), **Ann Hughes,** *The Causes of the English Civil War* (Macmillan 1991) and **Anthony Fletcher's** massively researched *Outbreak of the Civil War* (Arnold 1981). In addition, the serious student should read at least one of the publications by **Conrad Russell.** His revision of some earlier interptetations is characterised by its measured tone and balanced argument. Moreover his emphasis on the need to consider developments in Britain as a whole has introduced a new dimension and a genuinely original approach to the study of the period. His major work in recent years has been *The Fall of the British Monarchies, 1637-42* (Oxford 1991) but students may gain some awareness of his work from some of the collections of essays discussed below.

The approach to war and the political factions involved is addressed by **J.H. Hexter,** *The Reign of King Pym* (Cambridge, Mass. 1941). Again the interpretation has been challenged but the book remains of interest. There has been much debate about the emergence of different parliamentary groups, but there is no authoritative study of the presbyterian and independent groups. However, the issue is addressed by Derek Hirst, and in studies of the Army by **Austin Woolrych -** *Soldiers and Statesmen* (Oxford 1987) - and **Mark Kishlansky.** Kishlansky's argument in his *Rise of the New Model Army* (Cambridge 1980) that religion played little part in motivating the New Model remains controversial. Parliamentary factions have also been studied in depth in **David Underdown,** *Pride's Purge* (Oxford 1971) and **Blair Worden,** *The Rump Parliament* (Cambridge 1974). The best study of the royalist groups is **Ronald Hutton,** *The Royalist War Effort* (London 1981). An alternative approach to the Civil War is offered by local studies. Most counties have been investigated, and the list is far too long to be included in full here. However, **R.C. Richardson's** *Debate on the Civil War Revisited* (Routledge 1991) lists most of them, as well as being a useful introduction to the historiography of the period. An excellent survey is provided by **John Morrill's** *Revolt of the Provinces* (2nd ed. London 1980) which deals with the importance of local loyalties and neutralism in the Civil Wars.

Many attempts have been made to study radicalism and the role of the population as a whole. The attitudes of ordinary citizens were studied by Derek Hirst, with **Brian Manning's** *English People and the English Revolution* (London 1976) and **David Underdown's** *Revel, Riot and Rebellion* (Oxford 1985) developing the issues more fully. Radical groups are outlined in **Frances Dow's** *Radicalism in the English Revolution, 1640-1660* (Blackwell 1985) and analysed in **J.F. McGregor and B. Reay eds.** *Radical Religion in the English Revolution* (Oxford 1984). **Christopher Hill's** monumental *World Turned Upside Down* (Penguin 1975) is vastly informative. There are many excellent, and some over-enthusistic studies of the Levellers. One of the most accessible and balanced surveys is **Howard Shaw,** *The Levellers* (Longman Seminar Studies 1973).

A final category of recommended reading is defined by the type of publication rather than content. There are a number of useful collections of primary sources. **H. Tomlinson and D. Gregg,** *Religion and Society in Revolutionary England, 1640-60* (Macmillan 1989) includes a useful introductory commentary, while **Ann Hughes,** *Seventeenth Century England,* Vol. I (Open University 1980) limits comments to specific information about the sources. Many students also find biographies to be a useful way of studying the period. **Pauline Gregg's** *Freeborn John* (Dent 1986) is the best biography of John Lilburne. **Charles Carlton** has produced biographies of *Laud* (London 1987) and *Charles I* (London 1983). The most charismatic figure, however, appears to be Oliver Cromwell. Of the many accounts of his life, **Christopher Hill's** *God's Englishman* (1970) remains highly readable, while **Barry Coward's** *Oliver Cromwell* (Longman 1991) is clear and balanced. A recent publication by **D. Smith,** *Oliver Cromwell* (Cambridge 1993) uses primary sources to construct a biographical account. There is also an excellent collection of essays edited by **John Morrill** entitled *Oliver Cromwell and the English Revolution* (Longman 1990) which highlights particular aspects of Cromwell's life and career. The historiography of the period includes many collections of this kind. **Conrad Russell's** *Origins of the Civil War* (London 1973) and **John Morrill's** *Reactions to the English Civil War* (Macmillan 1982) contain contributions by many of the historians named here, and provide relatively easy access for students who already have a grasp of the main issues, and outlines of the major arguments and debates. Other essay collections such as **Russell's** *Causes of the Civil War* (Oxford 1990), **Morrill's** *Impact of the Civil War* (Collins and Brown 1991) and *Nature of the English Revolution* (Longman 1993) are equally useful. Although written by a single historian, their chapters address different issues and summarise debates in such a way that they can be used in separate sections. For students who have a heavy workload and find it difficult to work through books in a coherent way, these collections offer a user-friendly introduction to wider reading. A similar function is performed by articles and journals. There is clearly no space here to itemise separate articles, but the journal *History Today* has sought to encourage debate for many years, and a look through back numbers for the last decade would reap a rich and accessible harvest for those interested in extending their knowledge of the period.

Index

Army plots 33, 49
Assembly of Divines 8, 88, 105,
    109

Baptists 105, 111, 118
Bedford, Duke of 5, 33, 37
Berwick, Treaty of 5, 29
Bishops 28, 43-5, 50, 68, 105
Bishops' Wars 5, 27, 72

Church, reform of the 2, 4, 5,
    30, 43-45, 47-8, 69, 88,
    105
Charles I (actions) 29-31, 49,
    51, 52, 54, 84-5, 88, 92-3,
    97, 117, 130, 135
Cromwell, Oliver 9, 64, 70, 74,
    85, 87, 90, 91, 92, 108,
    110, 111-12, 114-5,
    116-7, 120-1, 128-30,
    132-3, 134

Digby, Lord George 43-4, 45,
    85, 92, 98
Edgehill, Battle of 7, 63, 66, 87
Essex, Earl of 8, 62, 63, 64, 85

Fairfax 8, 63, 72, 76, 83, 85, 89,
    97, 111, 115
Five Members, arrest of 7, 47,
    53-4

Grand Remonstrance 7, 53

Hampden, John 5, 37, 87
Haselrig, Sir Arthur 31, 116
Heads of the Proposals 9, 115

Holles, Denzil 31, 37, 110-11,
    112, 115-16, 134
Hotham, Sir John 7, 54-5, 72,
    76, 78, 83
Hyde, Edward (Clarendon) 31,
    42, 45, 47
    and royalists 47-9, 65,
    71, 73

Independents 8, 105, 107-8,
    115-16
Ireland (Irish) 7, 51-2, 85, 89,
    97
Ireton, Henry 9, 68, 70, 110,
    112, 113, 114-5, 120, 130

Laud, William 4, 28, 31, 32
Levellers 8, 9, 104, 106-7, 113,
    117-21
Localism 74-6 (Clubmen 96-7)
Long Parliament 6, 37, 50

Marston Moor, Battle of 8,
    89-90
Militia Bill / Ordinance 7, 53, 54
Multiple kingdoms 23-4, 30,
    143-4

Naseby, Battle of 8, 92-3
Neutralism 72-4, 94-7
New Model Army 8, 9, 83, 92-3,
    94, 96, 104, 106, 107-8,
    110-14, 117-21, 128, 130
Newcastle, Earl of 7, 63, 64, 72,
    83, 85, 89, 98
Newcastle Propositions 9, 97,
    109, 115

Nineteen Propositions 7, 55, 67

Oxford Negotiations 8, 63, 64, 72

Petition of Right 33, 37
Popery (Catholic) 4, 30, 32, 43-4, 52
Prerogative Courts 6, 32, 40
Presbyterian(ism) 2, 9, 43-4, 50-1, 88, 90-1, 106, 109, 115-16
Pride's Purge 9, 132-3
Prince Rupert 63, 64, 84, 85, 87, 89, 92-3, 94, 98
Puritan 32, 68, 69, 70-1
Pym, John 5, 8, 30, 31, 36-7, 38, 40, 49, 52-3, 54, 55, 83, 86, 87-8, 98
(and the opposition 34-9)
Queen Henrietta Maria 3, 40, 62

Radicals (and Separatists) 90, 104-8, 112, 113-14, 117-22

Ripon, Treaty of 6, 30
Root and Branch 32, 44, 47, 50-1
Saye and Sele 37, 116
Scots (also Covenanters) 8, 31, 37, 40, 48, 50, 83, 85, 87-8, 89, 90, 91, 97, 106, 109-10, 128
Second Civil War 9, 104, 121, 127, 128, 129-30
Self-denying Ordinance 8, 91-2
Ship Money 5, 6, 31, 40
Short Parliament 29, 31, 37
Slingsby, Sir Henry 27, 28, 44-5

Ten Propositions 6, 42
Three Resolutions 4, 31
Triennial Act 6, 32, 42

Uxbridge Negotiations 91

Wentworth, Sir Thomas and Earl of Strafford 4, 6, 28, 32, 40-1